Sr/Va-74

BUDGERIGARS
A
COMPLETE
GUIDE

STAN and
BARBARA MOIZER

Foreword by Alf Ormerod

MEREHURST PRESS

— LONDON —

Published 1988 by Merehurst Press
5 Great James Street
London WC1N 3DA

ISBN 0 948075 64 3

Editor: Lesley Young
Designer: Carole Perks
Typeset by Filmset
Colour separation: Fotographics Ltd, London-Hong Kong
Printed in Portugal by: Printer Portuguesa Industriagrafica LDA

Photo credits: Colour photographs are by Angela Moss. Black and white
photographs are by the authors, with additional pictures from the following
(on pages indicated): Ardea UK Ltd 142, J. Benson 134, Camera Press 102,
136, G. Clarke 72, J. Densley 130, Fox Photos 103, A. Francis 56, A.A.
Kent 21 bottom, Harry Lacey 67, 88 bottom, 109, 111, D.B. Nicholls 41,
Portsmouth and Sunderland Newspapers Ltd 48, Southern Aviaries 15,
135, Tony Tilford 20, 21 top, 35, 37, 43, 69 (both), 79 bottom, 113 bottom,
120, 138.

Acknowledgments: The authors would like to thank the following for
giving permission for their birds to be photographed: Steve Amos and
Ron Thumwood, Don Ashby, Jeff Attwood, Harry Bryan, Eric and Mike
Lane, Aubrey Punter and Bill Saundry. Gratitude is also expressed to all
who helped in the preparation of this book, including the American
Budgerigar Society, Dr John Baker, A. R. Bayliss, Arthur Bracey, Ray
Brown, the UK Budgerigar Society, Sherrill Capi, Graham Clarke, B. H.
Coles BV Sc. MRVS, Stephen Dew, Framed Philatelics, Rodney Harris,
Bernard Kellett, Linden Artists (Steve Lings and Brian Watson), Les
Lockey, Angela Moss, Alf Ormerod, Cyril Rogers and Graham Tann.

CONTENTS

Foreword

I have known Stan and Barbara Moizer for a number of years and feel sure it would be difficult to find a couple more dedicated to the hobby of breeding and exhibiting budgerigars. Between them they have had many years of practical experience and they are both very actively engaged in helping in the administration of the Budgerigar Society. Their intimate knowledge of the budgerigar fancy is aptly demonstrated in this book which is laid out in an easy to follow alphabetical style.

Newcomers will find a fund of information on all aspects of the hobby in this book, written in simple language and carefully cross referenced. Beginners who follow the advice on birdrooms, husbandry and breeding will have a sound basis from which to start. All aspects of exhibiting, the status rules, and show procedure have been meticulously covered to ensure that the relative newcomer can understand the path he should follow on the road to success in the show scene. With this book as his guide and with the patience and dedication that is so necessary in this hobby, there is no reason why he should not eventually begin to breed the outstanding specimens which are the aim of every serious breeder.

The budgerigar has changed a great deal over the years from the wild birds first brought over from Australia – and they are still changing. A book which brings the knowledge of all these changes up to date is a necessity and this book succeeds in that object.

For the experienced fancier, the book gives an opportunity to compare the various recommendations of the authors with his own routine and perhaps he will find that some of the ideas can be blended in to advantage with his own methods.

Whether the reader is simply a bird lover or a dedicated breeder and exhibitor, he will be delighted with the superb colour photographs of some of today's leading exhibition budgerigars; pictures which demonstrate the features so desirable in top show birds throughout the world.

I have read through this book several times and have no hesitation in recommending it to anyone who is interested in these little birds which have given me so much pleasure over so many years and have been the means of making friends in every corner of the globe. I hope it will serve to introduce many newcomers to our great hobby as well as supply new information to all experienced fanciers for whom a new book on budgerigars is a welcome occasion.

ALF ORMEROD

Introduction

Budgerigars are beautiful birds. They are available in myriad colours and pattern combinations; they are comparatively easy to manage and to breed; they adapt to almost any climatic conditions; they make affectionate and absorbing pets. Small wonder that these colourful parakeets have become so universally popular.

It was not always so. Until this century, they were virtually unknown outside their native Australia. When that country was discovered by Captain James Cook in 1770, one of the wonders reported was flocks of tiny parrots, so great in numbers that when they flew overhead they blotted out the sun for miles, and when they alighted on the branches of dead trees their brilliant green plumage gave the impression that the tree had been instantly resurrected and had broken into leaf.

Budgerigars were introduced to England by John Gould in 1840 and soon afterwards a few arrived in America. By the late 1880s, dealers were importing hundreds of thousands of pairs into Europe until, in 1894, the Australian government put a ban on the export of parakeets.

By this time, enthusiasts all over Europe were beginning to breed budgerigars and were so successful that the Australian ban had very little effect on the budgerigar population.

At first, all the birds were of the basic light green variety, but in 1870 the first colour mutation appeared in Belgium, causing quite a sensation. It was described as a pure yellow bird with red eyes, and is presumed to have been a lutino. At the same time, yellow birds with black eyes and pale wing markings appeared. The breeders knew nothing of sex-linkage at that time and the lutino was 'lost', but the black-eyed yellow variety was established.

Stories began to circulate of a budgerigar of incredible beauty. It was described as having a pure white face with a smooth, sky blue body. It remained but a legend until, in 1910, two skyblues were shown at a bird show at the Horticultural Hall, London.

With the advent of the blue series birds, the Royal House of Japan became interested in budgerigars and were reputed to have paid astronomical sums for pairs of blue birds. Japanese nobility started the fashion of giving these lovely blue and white birds as 'love tokens' and soon the fashion had spread to anyone who could afford the high prices being charged.

In 1927 the Japanese government banned the importation of budgerigars, but by this time the Japanese were breeding the birds themselves, and to this day, Japan has a strong following of budgerigar fanciers, and two national budgerigar associations.

After the skyblues came the dark greens which, when mated with the skyblues produced cobalts, and then, as the hobby passed out of the hands of the few into the realms of the ordinary fanciers, the mutations multiplied until today's enormous variety was achieved.

This book has been produced to cover all aspects of interest in the budgerigar. Its alphabetical arrangement of subject should allow anyone to find an item of interest very speedily. Thus, the owner of a new pet who wishes to teach it to talk can turn immediately to *TALKING* and will find comprehensive instructions, the newcomer to showing budgerigars will find all he needs to know listed under *SHOW PROCEDURE, NEST FEATHER SHOWS, OPEN SHOWS* or any other point on which he is unsure. For the experienced breeder wishing to renew or equip his birdroom, there are entries on *EQUIPMENT, BIRDROOMS, FLIGHTS* and many other subjects of interest. Anyone who has fallen under the spell of this most enchanting of birds will find this to be a book of absorbing interest.

A

ACCESSORIES

In addition to the birdroom or aviary, a number of items are required for breeding budgerigars. Some, such as seed hoppers and water fountains, will be in use throughout the year. Others, such as nest boxes, blocks and finger drawers for feeding soft food mixtures, are used only during the breeding season. Collectively these are known as accessories, but the most important items will be dealt with individually under the appropriate headings throughout the book.

ADDITIVES

This term is generally used to describe anything which is provided for the birds in addition to their normal food requirements (see *FEEDING*). It covers a huge range of products available from most good pet stores. A large number of these are added to the drinking water, but it cannot be stressed too strongly that when anything is added to the birds' drinking water, they have no choice but to take it, whereas if it is offered in a dry state they can ignore it if it is not wanted. Nature is often wiser than the breeder and the birds usually seem to know what is good for them and what is unnecessary.

One essential additive is iodine. This can be given in the form of iodine blocks which have the additional benefit of providing the birds with something to tear to pieces — which they undoubtedly enjoy. Iodine blocks can be obtained in small sizes intended for pet cages or those sold for the pigeon trade, which are ideal for use in budgerigar flights or breeding cages.

Various *vitamin supplements* are available, but care must be taken not to overdose with any particular vitamin. Carefully check the ingredients of any of the multi-vitamin products and do not give any other product containing a similar ingredient. Most products sold for babies and young children are harmless to budgerigars. A good rule of thumb amount is that suggested for the smallest babies. If this is then added to the drinking fountain, the dilution results in a suitable dosage. Baby tonics can also be given in the same manner, but these should not be necessary if a good basic diet is provided. (See *MINERALS* and *VITAMINS*.)

ADDLED EGGS

Originally fertile, the embryos in these eggs die in the very early stage — before the seventh or eighth day. Research has shown that the reason for this is frequently the presence of bacteria which have been absorbed through the shell. The egg takes on a dark tinge and when opened has quite a foul smell. The bacteria can be transferred to the eggs from the hands of the breeder, and for this reason the less the eggs are handled, the better. (See also *INCUBATION*.)

AGE

When buying a budgerigar as a pet, it is most important to check that it is a young bird because it is very difficult to tame or teach an adult bird to talk. In the normal varieties, the greens, blues, greys, etc., it is simple to tell if a budgerigar is under three months old, by observing the front of the head. Until the baby budgerigar has been through its first moult (usually between three and four months old), it has a series of *striations* across the top of the head from above the eyes. These birds are known as *barheads*. This method of deciding age cannot be used with varieties which have no markings, such as albinos and lutinos.

Another method of checking is to look at the eyes. For at least the first three months of their lives, the baby budgerigars have no whites around the pupils of their eyes. The pupil, black in the case of normals and deep red or plum coloured in albinos, lutinos, fallows and lacewings, is all solid colour with no white around the outside. There are exceptions to this rule,

A barhead budgerigar at 14 weeks of age. The bars, or striations, on the front of the head are just beginning to disappear.

The head of an adult budgerigar has no bars.

unfortunately. The recessive pied and dark-eyed clear varieties never develop the white iris rings around the pupils even in adulthood.

For breeding purposes it is always wise to buy *close-rung* birds. The ring will give the code number of the breeder and the year in which the bird was rung. If a bird is over three years old, while it might breed, there is always a doubt, and in any case it will not continue to breed in later years.

The average age of a budgerigar in the wild is probably about two or three years. A pet bird, however, can live well into its teens if well looked after.

AILMENTS AND DISEASES

In general, budgerigars are healthy little creatures and most live their whole lives without suffering from any disease, but, as with all livestock, they are subject to a number of ailments and, being such small creatures, have not a great deal of resistance to illnesses. Prompt attention is very important. The first sign of trouble is usually finding a bird roosting on both feet with its head tucked under its wing. Pet owners should be aware that it is *normal* for a bird to perch on *one* foot with its head tucked under its wing. If the plumage is fluffed out and the droppings are loose and watery, or green and slimy, it is a sure sign that all is not well. The bird should be caught up at once and

examined for injury. If none is obvious, then it should be put into either a hospital cage, or a show cage which can be placed near heat. If a hospital cage is used, the thermostat should be set at 29-32°C (85-90°F). If a hospital cage is not available then the show cage or a similar cage should be placed in front of a fire, on top of the central heating boiler, or in any place which is both draught- and fume-free. Gas appliances are not advised. Do not put the cage where the bird will be too hot, see *HOSPITAL CAGE*. In addition to drinking water, a shallow bowl of water should be placed near the cage to provide humidity.

If the illness is only minor, the most effective treatment is heat alone.

If the droppings are loose or green, very often the condition can be cured simply by substituting strong cold tea (without milk or sugar) for drinking water. This has an astringent effect and is soothing when the alimentary system has been inflamed for any reason. There are several proprietary brands of medicines available for the treatment of *diarrhoea* and *enteritis* and these should be used as directed on the bottle or packet. It is wise to check that these medicines have a fresh smell and have not been in stock for a long time in the pet store.

Anal prolapse is another distressing condition from which

breeding hens can suffer. This very seldom occurs if the seed provided during the breeding season is mixed with a very small amount of cod liver oil emulsion (see *FEEDING*). This condition is usually caused by the bird attempting to expel either a soft-shelled egg or a particularly large egg. Very rarely it can be the result of *constipation*.

The symptoms are fluffed feathers, tail held high, swelling around the vent, giving the appearance of the bird being 'blown up', while in severe cases part of the intestine may protrude from the vent.

The bird should be removed from the breeding cage and caged alone, the vent washed with a mild solution of disinfectant in warm water and then smeared with a mild disinfectant jelly or cream. If any intestine is protruding, this can be *very, very* gently pushed back into place. First wash your hands really thoroughly, then smear a finger liberally with a lubricating jelly or cream, then gently try to manoeuvre the protruding part back into place. If an egg can be felt, the bird should be put back into the cage and kept warm until the egg is passed. The bird should be given a few days' rest alone and its seed mixed with a minute quantity of cod liver oil, or liquid paraffin. It is advisable that this bird should not be used for breeding purposes until the following breeding season and then that a careful watch should be kept.

Coccidiosis is said to be a rare disease in budgerigars, but it occurred at one time in one of the authors' aviaries. The first sign was pink drops of liquid, about the size of a thumbnail, on the floor of the flight. A bird looked sick and was taken into the warm. The droppings were pink, as though a small amount of blood was present. They were pure liquid with no solid at all. The bird did not seem fluffed up as is normal with sick birds, but it was not eating and seemed lethargic. Within hours another had evinced the same symptoms. By the following morning, four more were in the same condition. A vet, called in, could not give an explanation, but took some of the liquid droppings for examination. Then the first bird to show the signs died. The body was taken to the vet without delay and the following day coccidiosis was diagnosed. The whole flock was treated with sulphadimidine and although about twenty began to show blood in their droppings, there were no more deaths. The sick birds recovered and there seemed to be no loss of fertility in the stock at the next breeding season. The birds were moved temporarily and the whole aviary stringently cleaned and disinfected before they were allowed back in.

Coccidia is a parasite which lays eggs in the intestines and penetrates the mucous lining. The eggs, called *oocysts* are passed in the droppings and can be picked up and swallowed by another bird. They multiply in the gut and eventually produce more oocysts. Because of the budgerigar's habit of eating old droppings, this cycle makes the disease very infectious within the stud.

FRENCH MOULT is the most perplexing and exasperating disease which affects budgerigars. This condition is dealt with under its own heading.

'*Going light*' is another perplexing condition which causes a great deal of concern among breeders. It is used to describe a budgerigar which, although apparently fit and eating well, continues to lose weight until the breast bone can be felt, sharp and without its normal covering of muscle and fat. Without treatment, the bird eventually dies.

Research into this condition has revealed that in the majority of cases, the villi, which are fine projections in the intestine, have become shorter, or have fused together, and this prevents the bird from absorbing the nutrients from the seed it eats. Tests have indicated that this condition can often be caused by allergies to certain foods, some possible sources being soaked oats, hard boiled eggs, or some of the more exotic seeds. It is recommended that birds going light should be given a very simple diet of plain canary seed, greenfood and pure water. An antibiotic is available to treat this condition, but it would be necessary to continue the treatment for the rest of the bird's life. Since it is not recommended that these birds should be used for breeding, and they would need to be caged separately, this seems impractical. However, pet owners could try to keep their birds healthy by offering a plain diet and by dosing with the antibiotic, sodium cromoglycate. As with any antibiotic, it is wise to seek advice from an experienced veterinarian on dosage. Many vets are the first to admit that they do not have great knowledge of treating small birds, but information is available from Liverpool University where much of the research into diseases in budgerigars has been carried out.

Vomiting in budgerigars is usually caused by a disease known as *trichomoniasis*. Owners of pets should not confuse this with the very normal behaviour of *regurgitating seed*. Vomiting is far more violent and usually results in the feathers above and below the beak becoming matted. This disease can be transmitted to other birds by beak to beak contact, which includes feeding chicks. An effective treatment is the antibiotic soluble emtryl, at the rate of one level teaspoon per 3·8 litres (1 gal). The solution should not be kept for more than three days. Excess dosage can be dangerous, therefore the amount should not be exceeded and the treatment given for seven days. Even though the vomiting has ceased, the treatment should be continued for the full seven days to prevent a resistance being built up to the antibiotic.

Fungi are the cause of *aspergillosis* and *candidiasis*. Fungi are airborne spores which land mainly on vegetable matter and cause mould to form. If you leave a moist loaf of bread around for a day or so, you can watch the moulds forming. The best prevention of fungal disease in your budgerigars is to keep their surroundings clean and dry and to remove all moist food or greenfood which has not been eaten the same day. Candidiasis usually occurs in the mouth or crop. The mould,

mixed with dead tissue, builds into a cheese-like mass which partially blocks the organ. Birds are usually treated with fungicidal antibiotics, but very often the diagnosis is not made until the condition has progressed too far for a cure to be effected.

The *aspergillus* fungus affects the air sacs and lungs of the bird, but provided that the bird is fit and vigorous, it should be able to overcome the disease before it reaches dangerous proportions. A vet may well advise treatment with an antibiotic, but this should not be given without expert advice.

Other diseases caused by fungus spores are *skin lesions*, such as *ringworm*. The signs to look for are loss of feather, exposing the skin which looks grey and scaly, or moist and yellow, and covered with a film which can be removed to show the skin slightly spotted with blood. The budgie is likely to scratch or rub the spot until it is raw and bleeding if it is not treated. Treatment with an anti-fungal cream is essential and must be continued until every trace of the lesion has disappeared. (See also *CHLAMYDIA* and *MEDICINES.*)

ALBINOS
The albino is a variety of budgerigar which appears to be pure white. It is, in fact, a blue series bird which is carrying the *albino factor*. This factor has the effect of removing all colour from the bird. The eyes are deep red with a white iris ring, and the feet and legs are fleshy pink.

AREA SOCIETIES
England, Wales and Scotland are divided into 10 area societies. Each sends two delegates to meetings of the General Council of the Budgerigar Society. Although autonomous, the area societies remain very much within the structure and guidelines laid down by the Budgerigar Society. They produce their own magazines and offer various prizes, both for open competition and to their own members. These include rosettes, trophies and cash prizes. The area societies administer their own

regions and issue to their members individual code numbers which cannot be duplicated. Membership of the area society allows members to purchase closed coded rings from the Budgerigar Society without the necessity of joining the parent body. The area societies hold regular meetings for members and for delegates of the local societies which are affiliated to them.

AUTOMATIC WATERING SYSTEM

Probably the most time-saving equipment which can be installed in a birdroom is an automatic watering system. It cuts out the necessity for drinking fountains and the daily chore of filling them, and ensures that the drinking water is always fresh. This system, which is widely used in the USA, consists of a pressure-reducing valve. This is a unit which is connected to the domestic water supply and reduces the mains water pressure. The water is routed to the cages and flights via a black PVC tube. (Black tubing is used to prevent any growth of algae which would occur in a transparent tube.) Tee pieces are used to supply the individual cages and flights. At the end of each tube there is a drinking outlet for the birds. This consists of a non-returnable valve with a stem which is moved by the birds. When the stem moves from

the central position, pure, fresh tap water is released. Budgerigars are very inquisitive and learn how to operate this system of water supply very quickly. When it is newly installed, it usually takes less than an hour for them to discover that pressing the valve delivers their water supply.

Two possible sources of danger, which should be watched for, are that the room should always be above freezing point, otherwise, just as in any water supply, the tiny pipes could freeze, and if for any reason, such as rebuilding, you need to break down the system, care must be taken to check, once it has been re-assembled, that it is fully operative again. To do this, press down the centre stem at each outlet to make certain that the water is running freely. It takes so little time to do this that it is a good idea to make it part of your daily routine. It is not necessary to check each individual outlet every day — just one from each run of piping would be quite sufficient. (See also *WATER*.)

AUTOPSY

When an unknown disease affects number of budgerigars in a flock, pointing to the likelihood of it being an infectious disease, unfortunately the most accurate diagnosis usually depends upon a detailed autopsy.

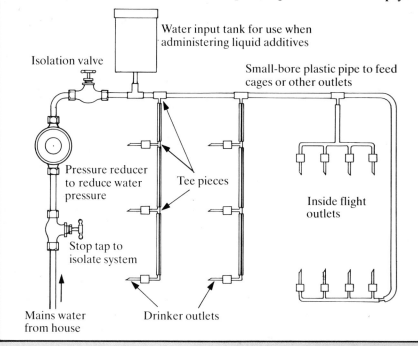

Water input tank for use when administering liquid additives

Isolation valve

Small-bore plastic pipe to feed cages or other outlets

Pressure reducer to reduce water pressure

Tee pieces

Inside flight outlets

Stop tap to isolate system

Mains water from house

Drinker outlets

An automatic watering system as seen on page 21.

Birds which have been dead for six hours or more are seldom of use for diagnosing bacterial disease. The fancier should therefore try to provide the veterinary surgeon with birds which appear to be in the terminal stages of the illness. Although this may seem harsh, and a breeder is always loath to lose birds which may well be those he most prizes, it is better to sacrifice one or two birds, which in any case seem unlikely to recover, than to lose a large part of the stud through an undiagnosed disease.

The more autopsies that are carried out, the more is learned about the causes of death and disease in our birds. Anyone who experiences a number of unexplained deaths, is advised to take some of the dead birds to the local vet for a post mortem, and the sooner after death these can be taken, the more likely is the vet to be able to pinpoint the cause.

One of the authors had an experience at one time which impressed upon him the importance of autopsies. One bird died, then another. He was unhappy about losing birds, but since they do suffer from heart attacks, strokes and most of such similar diseases in humans, he accepted the losses. When more died he suspected some form of poisoning. All the seed in stock was discarded and new supplies brought in. Every inch of the birdroom was checked for possible mice infestation and the birds were observed diligently. Still no clue was found: the birds appeared healthy and active and then they died. He took a couple along to the vet for an autopsy and what was found was specks of galvanising from the wire netting. Rust had penetrated underneath the galvanising of the wire mesh and the birds had picked it off. As soon as the wire netting had been changed, there was no further trouble.

AVIARIES

For bird lovers, a garden aviary can supply unending pleasure as they sit and watch the antics of budgerigars at play, marvelling at the variety of their colours. A very small outlay is needed to provide a garden with this focal point which will prove popular with family, friends and visitors alike.

Although planning permission is not required for building a garden aviary, it is both a wise and friendly gesture to check first with neighbours to be certain that there will be no objection to the noise of the birds.

The simplest and most basic type of garden aviary consists of an open flight fitted with sleeping quarters. A rigid framework is covered with wire netting or weldmesh.

Ideally, the aviary should have a sound concrete base with a slight slope to allow rain to run off, but if no base is to be provided, then the aviary needs to be pegged very firmly into the ground.

Once the flight is completed, secure sleeping quarters are necessary. They can be very primitive as long as they are secure, and could consist, virtually, of a four-sided wooden box, with the top covered, leaving the bottom open.

A window is needed at the back to allow light into the quarters and to allow you to see the birds. Two or three perches should be firmly fixed, lengthways, inside the box.

Another simple method of constructing sleeping quarters is to have a complete box with a window in the rear wall. The front, which faces into the flight, is made into an opening door to facilitate cleaning. Two entrance holes, about 5 cm (2 in) in diameter, need to be cut in the door to allow the birds to enter and leave the sleeping quarters. As with the four-sided box, perches need to be fitted firmly.

It is wise to clean, scrape and wash all floors weekly to avoid any build-up of droppings. Cleaning is made easier if sawdust or shavings are sprinkled on the floor of the sleeping quarters and if there is a concrete base to the aviary, a liberal spreading of coarse sand (washed clean of salt) both simplifies cleaning and enhances its appearance.

A flight 2-2.5 m (6-8 ft) long, a minimum of 0.9 m (3 ft) wide and 2 m (6 ft) high would be suitable for about 20 to 25 birds.

Diagram of a garden aviary with two flights.
1 Covered-in sleeping quarters (must be rain proof) 2 Glass window 3 Feed board 4 Doors 5 Aperture for birds to enter and leave 6 Perches 7 Food tray 8 Covered roof 9 Door to other flight 10 Safety porch 11 Outer door.

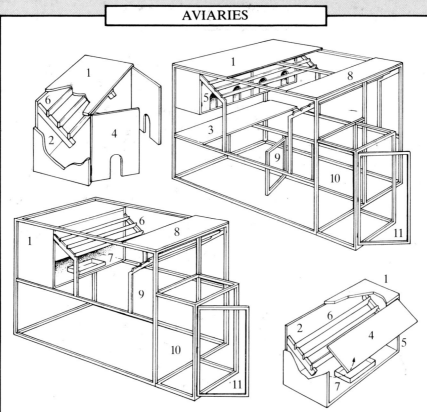

The framework can be made from 4 x 4 cm (1½ x 1½ in) timber or from hard plastic tubing. If timber is used it will be necessary to treat it with a *non-toxic* wood preservative prior to fitting the wire netting. The framework, both top and sides, should be totally covered with heavy-gauge wire netting or weldmesh to prevent the birds escaping and to protect them against cats, children and vermin. All the wire netting should be painted with black *bitumastic* paint, inside and out, as protection. The roof should be partially covered with a solid material to give the birds somewhere to shelter from the sun. It can be boarded and felted, or covered with an asbestos sheet or anything similar. The remainder of the roof needs to be covered with lightweight plastic to protect the budgerigars from the droppings of wild birds, which could be a source of infection.

Grass is not a good floor for the flight. It is very quickly eaten away by the birds and the ground, particularly under the perches, will become sour. If no floor has been built in, then it is a good idea to fork over the ground lightly, but regularly. The birds like to break up the newly forked ground, either for

enjoyment or when seeking grubs, insects and natural minerals. It is unwise to plant any type of shrub or tree inside the flight because it would quickly be stripped of bark and leaves. For safe access to the sleeping quarters or flight, a safety door will be necessary. A description of its construction will be found under *SAFETY DOORS*.

There are many forms of aviary which can be bought ready made, ranging from very simple to elaborate and decorative structures, but however well these might compliment the garden landscape, the welfare of the birds must be of primary importance. The rules given for a simple aviary must still be complied with.

It is very important that if you do not intend to breed birds you must never put anything resembling a nest box into the aviary as this would cause jealousy and fighting among the hens. Perhaps, in this case, it might be more sensible to keep only cocks, for there is seldom any squabbling among a flock of cocks. Once hens are introduced, however, especially when they are coming into breeding condition, then the hens are apt to fight for their partners and their territory.

14

Garden aviary with sleeping quarters.

Examples of outdoor aviaries. Ideally, they should have a sound concrete base or else be secured extremely firmly into the ground.

B

BARHEADS

This is a term used to describe young budgerigars before they have been through their first moult which usually takes place at the age of three to four months. Until they have moulted out their nest feathers, budgerigar chicks of the normal varieties have *bars*, or *striations*, across the front of their heads. Once the nest feathers moult out, the new feathers are of a clear colour, either yellow or white, depending on whether the bird is of the green or blue series.

BATHS

Although it is not essential for budgerigars to bathe, most enjoy it and it is good for them. It encourages them to preen their feathers which helps to give them the bloom that is essential for show winners. Care should be taken never to provide too deep a bath because the birds can drown in water over about 4 cm (1½ in) deep. The bowls must be removed once the birds have used them to prevent them being fouled by droppings and becoming a potential health hazard. For pet cages, plastic baths which fit on to the opening can be obtained and they will provide hours of entertainment for both pet and owner. If the pet bird is loath to enter a bath for the first time, it can be encouraged by putting at the far side any titbit of which it is fond — a piece of millet spray, greenfood or sweet apple will usually entice it in. Many pet budgies delight in bathing under a cold tap which has been left dribbling — but the owner must make absolutely certain that all doors and windows are closed and no hotplates are turned on (or still hot) before releasing his pet in the kitchen.

BEAKS

The beak does not become really hard until the budgerigar is about three weeks old. During this time it is most important that it should not be distorted by the accumulation of caked food. The beak should be examined daily and any trapped food should be removed gently with a blunt matchstick or toothpick. (See *UNDERSHOT BEAK*.)

BEGINNER

In the United States and several other countries, no beginner classes are scheduled and exhibitors go directly into novice classes. In some smaller shows in the UK this is also true and in this case it is permissible for beginners to enter the novice classes and then revert to beginner classes when these are scheduled. Much confusion arises from the fact that an exhibitor may remain a beginner for the rest of his life *if he never enters in open shows*.

The BS rule is that a beginner may

A plastic bath which fits over the opening to the budgerigar cage.

show in this section *either* for three years *or* until he or she has won four first prizes in *full* classes *at open shows — whichever is the longer period*. Full classes consist of at least seven exhibits shown by three different exhibitors and can be any age or breeder classes. For the purpose of counting these wins, one prize is counted for a win of a prize of best in section, provided three exhibitors are competing and there are seven exhibits in the line-up being judged.

BELLS

Although pet budgies love to ring bells, care must be taken to ensure that the clapper of the bell is very

A budgerigar with bell and mirror.

firmly fixed. Where the clapper is tiny and can be broken off, it has been known for the budgie to try to eat it — with disastrous results. With patience, a budgie can be trained to ring a bell when it wants something. A great deal of amusement can be caused by a budgie ringing its bell to have something which it has thrown out picked up from the floor. One little fellow used to empty a tray of hair grips by throwing them one by one onto the floor, and then ring his bell violently until someone picked them up and returned them to his tray. (See also *TOYS*.)

BEST OF COLOUR CERTIFICATES

These are similar to *challenge certificates*, but are awarded at shows at a lower patronage level, and for the purpose of obtaining a *champion bird certificate*, nine best of colour certificates, at least three of which must be won in adult classes, would be needed (or two challenge certificates and three best of colour certificates, or one challenge certificate and six best of colour certificates). Three best of colour certificates are equal to one challenge certificate. A best of colour certificate can be won with an unrung bird, but in this case the certificate would be marked to this effect and the certificate would not count towards a champion bird certificate. As with challenge certificates, the exhibitor must be a Budgerigar Society member, and have nominated BS on his entry form, to be eligible to win a best of colour certificate.

BIRDROOMS

Basically, a birdroom is an enclosed building plus flights. The building can be an existing shed, unused garage, or barn, or it can be something which is purpose-built as a birdroom. Whatever is used, there are certain basic requirements. The building must be weatherproof. Any leaking from the roof must be stopped before the building can be used. Other than the discomfort that this can cause the fancier, more important is the comfort, safety and hygiene of the birds. Water could seep into the nest boxes and literally drown the baby chicks, or it could soak the nesting material, causing discomfort and possibly serious illness in the hen. It might soak into materials which could cause moulds to be released into the air and inhaled by the birds. Every leak and potential leak must be eliminated.

The next task is to draw out a plan giving the location of cages, flights, storage area, windows and the entrance door into the birdroom. The drawings on page 25 show a suggested plan which can be followed if the building is being newly built, or modified where

The normal varieties

Normal dark green cock.

A violet budgerigar on a Capern's card. (These cards were issued by the makers of Capern's bird seed.)

Normal violet hen.

Magnificent normal grey cock with outstanding head qualities.

necessary for an existing building.

It is preferable that the birdroom and flights face south to catch all the warmth of any sun there is during the spring period when the youngsters are most likely to be using the flights. Flights facing north east should be avoided if it is humanly possible, as these would catch the coldest and most biting of the winter winds. Although budgies are hardy little creatures, they seem to have no instinct which tells them to shelter from cold winds.

If the birdroom is built of timber,

An extra coat at this time can do no harm and may save a deal of maintenance in the future. For your own comfort, that of the birds, and for long-term savings on heating, the interior of the birdroom should be insulated, including the roof. *Polystyrene* is not recommended for this purpose because mice could get into it and use it for nesting purposes. *Fibreglass* or *rockwool* makes life far too uncomfortable for rodents to want to make nests.

If openings are needed into the flights, these should be cut out

The authors' birdroom with its attached flight.

always try to allow for later expansion, for most fanciers find that they wish to expand their first birdroom as their interest, and their stock, grows. Even if a building is being adapted, it is often possible to plan judiciously so that extra space for banks of breeding cages can be left for the time when they will be needed, or an extra flight built on. Taking time to make plans, asking for advice from other fanciers and visiting other birdrooms pays dividends at this time.

The outside of the wooden building needs to be treated with a *non-toxic preservative* before any additional building is carried out.

before the shed is lined. Small bob-holes may be useful in winter to prevent draughts, but in hot months it is better to have as much ventilation as possible. (See *VENTILATION*.) The ideal solution is to cut holes 46 x 46 cm (18 x 18 in) and then keep them partially blocked during the winter.

Before lining the birdroom, all electrical wiring should be installed so that no cables are available for the birds to nibble. Now line the shed with a good quality 10 mm (⅜ in) plywood, laminated coated board, or other suitable material. All joints should be sealed with good-quality thick adhesive, so that, should *mites* ever become a problem, there would be no cracks and crevices for them to escape from disinfectants and sprays. A coat of white, or light-coloured emulsion over the lining of the birdroom will lighten the whole building. At this point, wooden frames should be built in, onto which breeding cages will later be built.

Cages are the next priority. In a small birdroom the same cages can be used for breeding cages, stock cages, show preparation and even for internal flights. Using 5 x 2.5 cm (2 x 1 in) batten, cut and screw this along the wall, then across the front. Next, panel in the floors/ceilings using plywood, with a piece of 5 x 2.5 cm timber, running from front to rear beneath the cage floor levels. The fronts of the cages can be produced in single units or as a block. Using 5 x 2.5 cm timber for all the uprights, and 13 x 2.5 cm (5 x 1 in) for the vertical pieces, will produce a frame which can be attached to the floors/ceilings to form a block of cages. A coat of white emulsion on the new timber both protects and enhances its appearance.

Wire cage fronts can be purchased from a number of suppliers who advertise in the birdworld press. The fronts have wires trimmed off flush at the top and bottom of the cross

The interior of a birdroom showing the pipes of its automatic watering system.

An outdoor aviary that would be suitable for housing budgerigars or a mixed collection of birds.

21

Winning champions

Opaline grey green cock displaying the short, wide neck called for by the standard of excellence.

Normal light green cock.

Normal skyblue cock.

A Capern's card showing a skyblue budgerigar.

wires, but a few of the wires are left longer for attachment to the wooden frames. Place the wire front against the frame and mark the places where the extended wires will be fixed, then drill a tiny hole, 2.5 cm (1 in) deep, in the centre of the front rail of the cage. Place the wires of the front into the drilled holes and press home, then repeat at the top of the cage. It is necessary to bend the wire cage front slightly to allow it to spring into position where it will now be perfectly secure.

Removable slides are now fitted between each cage. These can be made of plywood, sheet metal, hardboard, perspex, glass or wire attached to a wooden frame. Wire has the disadvantage of allowing the birds to squabble and pull out each other's feathers, or to perch on the wire sides of their cages, more interested in the occupants of the adjoining cages than in their own mates. Plywood, sheet metal and hardboard have the disadvantage of opacity, and therefore slides of glass or perspex are recommended. These give ease of cleaning and allow the birds to see the display and mating of their neighbours which acts as a stimulus.

When fixing the door to your birdroom you cannot be too *security* minded. It should be as substantial as possible. If using a padlock, it is worth while buying one made from toughened steel, with a good locking mechanism. Ensure that the hasp and staple are bolted to the frame with the heads protected. *Never* fit the hinges of the door on the outside, it is far too easy for someone to take out the screws or knock out the pins. The safest fastening for your outside door is a good-quality mortice lock. Develop good habits in security. Never leave the key in the door and once the birdroom is locked, keep the key in a safe place inside your house.

If there is space for a separate, but attached, storeroom, this is ideal. If not, try to keep as much equipment as possible off the floor so that if, by some unfortunate chance, mice should get into the birdroom, this will be spotted very quickly. Try to keep items in constant use in cupboards and avoid using cardboard containers because these become dust traps.

FLIGHTS, both inside and outside are now necessary and *HEATING* and *LIGHTING* need to be considered. They will be found under their own entries.

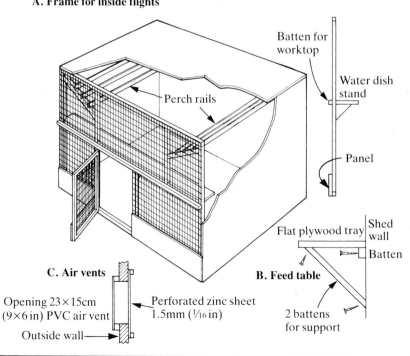

A. Frame for inside flights

Batten for worktop

Water dish stand

Perch rails

Panel

Flat plywood tray | Shed wall

Batten

C. Air vents

Opening 23×15cm (9×6 in) PVC air vent

Perforated zinc sheet 1.5mm (1/16 in)

Outside wall

B. Feed table

2 battens for support

BREEDERS' AWARDS

In most shows, awards are given for breeder, or current-year rung birds. To qualify for these, the bird must be wearing the closed, coded ring of the exhibitor, for the current year. It is always considered a greater achievement to win prizes with birds one has bred oneself, therefore breeders' awards are more highly prized than those for any age birds. This is recognised by donors of cups and trophies, who often stipulate that they should be given in the breeder section, and this stimulates the competition.

BREEDING CAGES

Basically there are two types of breeding cages in popular use. The *all-wire* cage is used widely in the United States and is gaining in popularity in the UK. It consists of a six-sided box made from flat panels of rectangular welded wire mesh. Sizes vary, but the average size is 76 cm wide x 61 cm high x 61 cm deep (30 x 24 x 24 in). All the edges are clipped together with special wire clips to ensure the rigidity and security of the cage. A door is cut out in the front, secured at one side with clips, and a door fastener is fixed to the other side. Two perches are fitted at about the halfway mark and the cage hung onto hooks fitted to the wall. A small gap is left between the bottom of one cage and the top of the one below and a sheet of paper inserted to catch the droppings. It is unhygienic and dangerous to allow droppings from one cage to drop into another, as disease or parasites can be spread very easily in this way. One drawback of this type of cage is that if a chick came out of the nest too early, as they often do, there would be no dry litter in which it could keep warm if the weather was particularly cold.

The conventional type of breeding cage, used by the vast majority of breeders in the UK, is virtually a wooden box with a wire front. The needs and comfort of the birds should be of prime concern, even if it means cutting down on the number of cages the breeder would like to have, and the *minimum* size recommended is 76 cm wide x 46 cm high x 46 cm deep (30 x 18 x 18 in). A board placed across the bottom front prevents husks and other debris from falling to the floor. The best position for the large access door is in the centre, as this enables the breeder to catch the birds more

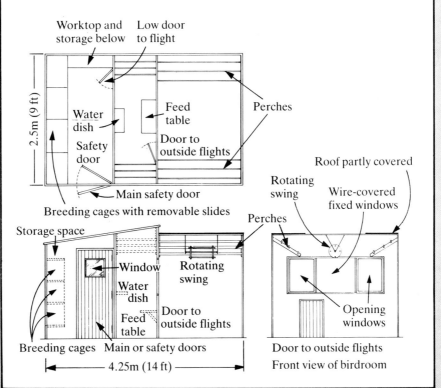

Diagram of a birdroom and flights.

Worktop and storage below — Low door to flight

2.5m (9 ft)

Water dish
Safety door

Feed table

Door to outside flights

Perches

Main safety door

Breeding cages with removable slides

Storage space

Window
Water dish
Feed table

Rotating swing

Door to outside flights

Perches

Breeding cages   Main or safety doors

4.25m (14 ft)

Roof partly covered

Rotating swing

Wire-covered fixed windows

Opening windows

Door to outside flights

Front view of birdroom

The opaline variety

A Capern's card
showing an opaline
light green cock.

Opaline light green
cock with excellent
opalescent wing
markings.

An opaline dark
green cock with
wing markings
showing an excess
of body colour.

Opaline cobalt cock.

A typical breeding cage.

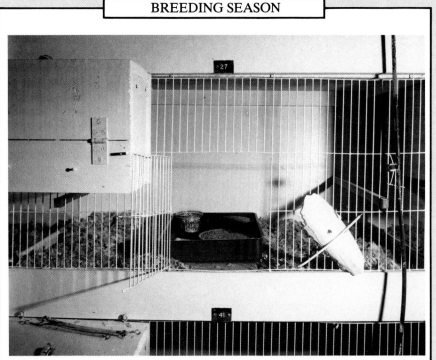

easily when necessary. From the point of view of cleanliness and attractiveness, it is recommended that the inside of the cage is painted with white, or pale-coloured emulsion paint. Nest boxes can be placed inside the cage or hung on the outside. If they are used on the outside, it is necessary to remove a small part of the wire to allow the birds access, and a small removable door should be fixed to close the opening in the wire front when the cage is not being used for breeding. Two perches are then fixed, preferably of 1.9 x 1.5 cm (¾ x ⅝ in) timber.

Cages are normally ranged in banks, with removable side panels, which allows them to be used as stock cages for weaning the youngsters, for steadying birds prior to the show season and for show preparation. These slides can be made from sheet metal, plywood, hardboard, stiff wire netting (though this could allow some squabbling between the pairs), glass or perspex. The latter two are favoured because they allow more light into the cages and allow the birds to see each other, which seems to be an advantage during the breeding season.

At one time, trays were fitted to the base of breeding cages to facilitate cleaning and changing and replenishing food containers, but they are seldom used now.

BREEDING SEASON

The most important time of the year is the breeding season. On this depends the success or failure you will achieve on the show bench in the coming season. When it should begin is a subject of much controversy, but if you are breeding birds for exhibition, and provided that you have provision for artificial lighting and heating in your birdroom, then late November is the most convenient time for pairing up the birds. This means that the first chicks will be emerging at the end of the year, ready for the new issue of rings on 1 January. Youngsters who are born early in the year have the opportunity to develop before the show season begins, and second-round chicks will also be independent by then, allowing you to clear and clean the birdroom before using some of the cages to house the show team.

Once you have selected your pair (see *PAIRING*), record the details of the colour, sex and ring number of both birds on the record card for that cage, put in the birds and leave them alone for two or three days to become acclimatised to their new surroundings. While you carry on filling the remainder of your breeding cages, or until all the birds with which you are satisfied have been paired up, watch to see there is no fighting between cock and hen.

They must be happy together for satisfactory results. Three days later the nest boxes can be attached to the breeding cages and the pairs allowed to enter them at will. In ten to fourteen days' time, the hens should begin to lay eggs. Just before laying commences, the droppings of the hen become enlarged, far more copious and wetter than at other times of the year. Eggs are then laid on alternate days and each chick normally hatches on the eighteenth day after the egg is laid.

During the *incubation period* the egg requires heat which the hen is able to provide if left in peace. Hens can be upset, and even leave their eggs, if they are constantly disturbed by the anxious breeder opening the nest box for innumerable checks. A wise thing to remember is that the breeding cage is the budgies' home — you are the intruder.

Establish a routine to build up the birds' confidence. Visit the birdroom twice a day, preferably at the same time each day. Carry out your inspection and feeding in a regular order. For example, begin at the entrance and work towards the exit, or vice versa, but always in the same order. By checking through one cage at a time, you will never miss any bird which appears distressed in any way. One important thing to remember whilst checking the nest boxes is that by *handling* the eggs, you can never make an infertile egg fertile, but *you can be the cause of a fertile egg failing to hatch*. One rule you must follow is never to handle eggs or chicks with cold hands; either warm them on a radiator, keep a bowl of hot water available, or even take a hot water bottle with you to make sure that your hands are kept warm. During nest box inspection, any chicks old enough and big enough should be rung. (See *RINGING A CHICK.*)

The next task is to replenish the seed pots, then soaked oats, greenfood or any other additives are distributed and, finally, the water drinkers are refilled. It is worth remembering that the hen is in a very warm environment in the nest box. If she were to emerge and drink newly supplied, icy-cold water, it could cause troubles. To avoid this it is wise to fill a bucket with water and leave it overnight so that it will have reached room temperature by the time it is used.

It is unhygienic to leave the heavy droppings from the hens in the breeding cages. They can become mouldy and are a breeding ground for bacteria. They should be removed at least once a week.

Finally, and every time, remember to sweep the floor and leave the birdroom tidy.

Unfortunately, the breeding season brings its problems. The nest box should be checked each day once chicks have arrived. If the hen is a 'dirty feeder' and manages to leave food around the face of the chick, this needs gently cleaning off with a piece of soft cloth and warm water, but be very careful as the chick is very weak when tiny and it would be easy to drown it with a very small amount of water. Ensure that no food is stuck inside the beak. If there is, it can be cleaned away, very gently, with a toothpick or matchstick. If it will not come off easily, it can be soaked off with a tiny amount of warm water.

Droppings do become stuck to the leg ring as the youngsters grow. This is not a major problem as it can be cracked free when the chick is about four to five weeks old, by the use of the thumb nail. Again, if it cannot be cleaned by this method, soaking in warm water will remove it.

If the chick's feet become fouled with droppings, it is a more serious matter and requires attention to prevent the feet becoming malformed. Wash the feet with warm water until all the dirt is cleaned away, dry gently with a clean cloth and, to prevent any recurrence of the problem, remove any wet droppings from the nest box and replace with clean, dry sawdust.

When checking the nest boxes, it is necessary to note whether all the chicks are being fed. Sometimes, for no apparent reason, the parents stop feeding one particular baby. Whether they have taken a dislike to it, or whether it does not call for food as loudly as the others in the

The cinnamons

Cinnamon light
green cock.

Two Capern's cards
showing cinnamon
cobalt and
cinnamon dark
green budgerigars.

Cinnamon cobalt
cock which shows
clearly how the
cinnamon factor
dilutes the body
colour.

Cinnamon skyblue
cock.

nest cannot be decided. There are occasions when a hen decides she will stop feeding a chick at a certain age, although she will continue to feed her younger offspring until they, too, reach the cut-off age. Unless action is taken, they will all die. In cases such as these, the chicks must either be transferred to another box and a foster mother, or must be hand fed which is tedious and time consuming. Wherever possible, the chicks should be transferred into a box where there are youngsters of a similar age. If left too long with parents who are not feeding, the chick will become too weak to call for food and will die. The chicks are accepted better if, before being put into the new box, they are rubbed with a little of the sawdust from the new box and the breeder holds them and any other chicks from the new box together, so that they will all share the same smell.

Occasionally a chick with a very *distended crop* is discovered. This is thought to be caused through poor feeding by the hen, but it could be that food has fermented and caused the crop to blow up like a balloon, or the cause might be that the nostrils have become jammed up with food and the baby has not realised it can also breathe through its mouth. Whatever the cause, prompt action is necessary if the chick is going to survive. First the nostrils should be examined, and if caked with food, this should be wiped off gently with a warm damp cloth, until they are free. Now the wind in the crop must be removed. The crop is pressed gently but firmly in an upwards direction and wind, sometimes together with a small amount of liquid, is expelled through the beak. These chicks will need watching more than others who appear to be well fed, because if the fault is incorrect feeding by the hen, wind may need to be expelled physically several times. Eventually the hen, usually a maiden, succeeds in feeding properly and no more gas is formed. If it is found that the condition persists for more than a few days and it is constantly necessary to 'wind' the chick, it

should be fostered to a good feeder. Sometimes it is a good plan to put a well-fed baby of the same age in with the hen who has been feeding badly, as such a baby seems able to teach the mother how to do the job properly, strange though it may seem.

Feather plucking is a problem which occasionally occurs. Some hens just pull out the fluffy down, but never touch the feathers. This can be ignored. Sometimes, however, the plucking can be far more serious, ranging from a few feathers at the back of the chick's head, through stripping the back and wings, to a situation where the chick is so viciously attacked that it is killed. Careful observation is called for to identify whether the hen or cock is the culprit and when one is certain, that bird should be removed from the breeding cage and the other partner left to bring up the youngsters. The youngster which has been damaged should have some soothing ointment smeared onto the broken area of skin. If it is only a matter of a few feathers having been pulled out and the skin left unbroken, that chick, and any others in the nest, can be sprayed with one of the proprietary anti-pecking liquids, or even with a strong-smelling perfume. Whichever is used, it is necessary to protect the chick's eyes whilst it is being applied.

Occasionally, an adventurous baby leaves the nest before it is fully feathered and before it is strong enough to withstand the environment outside the box. If, when found, it is chilled, do not place it straight back with the other chicks, but warm it first.

Sometimes the chicks are harassed by the cock once they have left the nest. There are several theories as to the reason for this. Sometimes the cock is trying to mate with his own baby daughters; sometimes the chicks interfere when the cock is trying to feed or mate with the hen; sometimes the chicks seem to worry at the cock to feed them continually. Whatever the cause, the cock may attack the youngster. It may only pull out flight feathers as the chick struggles to free itself from its bad-tempered father, but at other times the attack may be vicious and can end in the death of the chick. To avoid these problems, place a small box in a corner of the breeding cage, where the chicks can gather together in the same way as they did in the nest box. It is surprising how quickly this restores harmony and allows the chicks to remain safe and well fed.

A risky period is the time when the chicks are ready to be taken away from the parents. Make certain that they are more than 42 days old and observe that they are eating seed independently. Usually they will adapt to living with the other youngsters you have taken away without difficulty. On rare occasions, one chick is found which is not eating. If this is noticed within 48 hours of it being taken away, you can try putting it back in the cage with its parents, but you will need to sit somewhere away from the cage and watch for at least half an hour to ensure that neither parent attacks it. Provided the cock starts feeding the youngster, it is worth disturbing the hen to ensure that she has seen and accepted it before you leave the birdroom. Sometimes it is possible to persuade a pair with other chicks due to leave them shortly to accept the hungry chick, but never try this if the nest box is still up and until you have observed the reaction of the proposed foster parents.

Another problem which can occur in the nest box is a hen which sits too heavily on the chicks, causing their legs to splay out and the body to lie flat. Unless this is corrected soon after it first happens, it can result in permanent distortion of the legs, to such an extent that the youngster will be unable to perch or walk and will have to be destroyed. As soon as a chick with *splayed legs* is discovered, it should be treated by putting a split ring on the second leg and tying the two rings together with wool or soft string. The chick will be unable to walk properly and may appear distressed for a short time, but it will soon adapt to the new situation. The rings should be kept tied fairly tightly for ten days before the wool and split ring are removed. By this time, the soft little legs will have hardened to a degree and will be growing straight again.

BUFF

The term buff is given to coarse-feathered birds. Under a low-powered microscope, or a magnifying glass, it can be seen that these feathers have tiny 'hooks' on the ends. The bird also grows a thick layer of down, so that these birds appear to be larger than those with smooth feathers (generally called 'yellows'), but have been found more difficult to breed with.

The head of a buff feathered bird.

Although highly prized for the show bench, it is advised that a buff bird should not be paired with another buff, to avoid the production of double buffs which could eventually lead to infertile stock.

BUYING BUDGERIGARS

The newcomer to budgerigar breeding finds the purchase of his first stock a difficult matter. When? Where? How much? He is beset with queries. The best time for buying stock is around July and August. It is then that experienced fanciers are sorting out their year's stock and deciding which birds they can afford to dispose of and which they intend to keep. From the birds' point of view, it allows them to settle down into their new surroundings; in the autumn they will be able to moult out in the environment in which they will be breeding and they will get used to the new water supply and to the methods of husbandry of their new owner. The newcomer is advised to purchase his stock from an established breeder in his area, to whom he can then go back for advice should he run into any difficulties. If possible the first stock should be made up of six cocks and eight or nine hens. This will give the new breeder the chance of breeding from several pairs at the same time and allows for possible difficulties with some of the hens. Colour should not be important in these early stages, but very often the newcomer has already adopted a preference for a particular colour before he has begun. A very simple rule to follow, before the new breeder has a better understanding of genetics, is that if he starts with blue birds and then introduces one or more greens, eventually green will take over as the dominant colour. In the same way, if he starts with green and introduces grey, then grey will be the predominant colour in a short while. If opaline markings are introduced into a breeding room along with normals, opaline will become predominant, and if cinnamons are then introduced, they will 'take over'.

What should you pay for your first birds? If breeding for exhibition is your goal, then you will need to start with birds of reasonable quality. Perhaps the best guide would be that the bird should cost about the same price as 25 kg (55 lb) of budgerigar seed. If pet breeding is your goal then much lower priced stock can be used. In this case colour is a consideration as pet buyers prefer pretty colours. The *ideal age* for your first stock should be between six and ten months old. Birds at that age will be fully moulted out, you should be able to see their full potential, and you will not be buying old birds which might have vices for which you, as a raw beginner, would not be prepared.

One thing which is not advised is for beginners to go out and pay 'silly' prices for birds. Some beginners come into the fancy and are told that Mr X has the best birds in the country and that if they can buy from him, they, too, will reach the heights. They are led to believe that they can cut out years of hard work

and time spent learning the trade by spending huge amounts on their initial stock. This is absolutely untrue. If they know nothing about breeding budgerigars, then they will learn as much from breeding pets as they will from breeding from the most expensive birds in the country — and they will make as many mistakes. If they start with high price birds, in the first year they might be lucky and produce a few winners, but their lack of experience will soon show and, disillusioned, they may well leave the fancy for good. If their ambition is to breed exhibition birds, then they should start with exhibition birds, but they are beginners and it is a beginner's type of bird for which they should be looking for their first stock.

An experienced and reputable champion breeder will refuse to sell to a beginner birds which he knows are far too good to practise on.

C

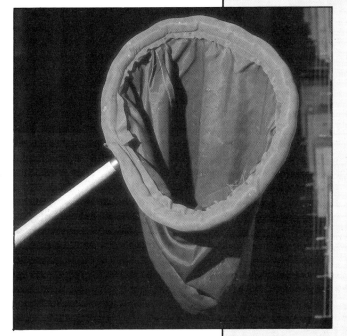

A catching net.

CAGES

Cages for pets are sold in all sizes and shapes. The first rule when buying a cage is that a bird flies from side to side and not vertically. The longer the cage the better for the bird, especially if it is to spend a great deal of time in it. Very high cylindrical cages, whilst they may add to the decor of your home, are unsatisfactory for budgerigars.

A useful accessory, which can be bought at the same time as the cage, is a cover for the base of the cage, which will catch any falling seed. Budgerigars, especially babies, love to scratch and scatter seed, and a base cover or tray can prevent a lot of vacuuming.

Show cages are a necessity for the potential exhibitor. These are small wooden boxes with wire fronts in which the bird can be transported to shows in safety and in which they must be shown. All show cages must comply with the Budgerigar Society's standard and must be fitted with their *ivorine label*. Newcomers should check this standard before exhibiting birds at shows which are run under BS rules.

BREEDING CAGES are dealt with under a separate heading.

CATCHING

To catch birds in an aviary, a catching net is an essential piece of equipment. When buying your first net, you should note the length of the handle. These are usually 30 cm (12 in) long, but if you are particularly short, or if your birdroom or flights are particularly high, then it is best to buy a net with a 46 cm (18 in) handle. To catch a bird, stand facing the bird you require, wave the net underneath the perch on which it is sitting to make it fly towards you and, keeping your eye upon it, swing the net smoothly, rather like an overhand shot in tennis, capturing the bird quite safely.

A pet bird can be captured easily in darkness. First close the curtains, making sure that there is no open fire, or that it is safely covered. Watch where the bird has landed, ask someone to switch off the light quite suddenly and the bird, surprised by the darkness, can be picked up with ease.

CHALLENGE CERTIFICATES

These certificates are awarded by the Budgerigar Society at shows to which they give their higher levels of patronage. At area society shows and at their own world championship shows, challenge certificates are awarded for both breeder and any age sections, whilst at championship shows both breeder and any age bird in each colour must compete for the same certificate.

These challenge certificates are highly prized by exhibitors and convey a certain amount of prestige to the winning bird. The name of the exhibitor, the show at which it was awarded, the judge's signature and, most important, the ring number of the bird, are recorded upon the certificate. No challenge certificate can be awarded to a bird unless the exhibitor is a member of the Budgerigar Society, has nominated BS on the entry form, and the bird is wearing a closed coded ring purchased through the Budgerigar Society.

At a show, the system through which the bird is chosen for this award is that each colour is judged throughout all the sections. The first prize winner of each colour is then placed before the judge who selects the best of those prizewinners. That bird is awarded the place of best of colour. The entry form is then consulted to ensure that the exhibitor is a member of the BS and has nominated accordingly. The bird is checked to ensure that it is rung, that the ring is a BS ring, that it has in no way been tampered with and that it is a current-year ring if the bird has been entered in breeder classes. If all these details are in order, the bird is awarded the challenge certificate; if not it is awarded the best of colour place, but the next-placed bird which complies with all the appropriate regulations is awarded the CC.

Challenge Certificates are awarded for the following varieties:

Normal green series (excl. grey green)
Normal blue series
Grey
Grey green
Opaline green series (incl. opaline grey green)
Opaline blue series (incl. opaline grey)
Normal cinnamon or greywing
Opaline cinnamon or opaline greywing green series
Opaline cinnamon or opaline greywing blue series
Lutino
Albino
Whitewing
Yellowwing
Dominant pied or clearflight
Recessive pied or dark eyed clear
Crest or tuft
Yellowface (excl. yellowface pieds)
Any other colour not otherwise competing for a certificate

CHAMPION

This is the highest status for exhibitors. It is the section from which most of the top award winners come because before an exhibitor reaches this status, he has usually spent many years of dedicated hard

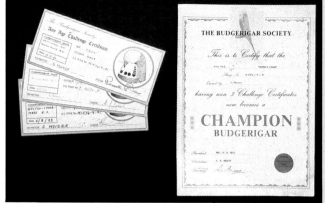

A prized champion bird certificate with the three challenge certificates needed to obtain it.

Opaline grey hen of challenge quality.

Challenge certificate winning opaline grey green cock.

work. It is possible, though far from advisable, for a person to show in the champion section when he first starts exhibiting, or at any time thereafter but once a person has shown in this section (unless it was because there was no lower section scheduled), he is unable to revert to a lower status, and it would be an extremely rare occurrence if such a person could keep any sustained success without the long period of apprenticeship which the rules allow. There is one exception to this rule which is that if a champion should cease to keep birds for a period in excess of five years and later returns to exhibiting, he will be able to enter one section lower, in this case the intermediate section, if he so wishes.

No person who keeps budgerigars at the same address as another showing in the champion section, is allowed to exhibit in a lower section.

In the USA the rules do not allow an exhibitor to show in champion classes until he has obtained the appropriate number of wins.

CHAMPION BIRDS
A budgerigar can become a champion bird by winning three *challenge certificates*, at least one of which must be won in adult classes. Alternatively, it can win three *best of colour certificates* in place of one or more of the challenge certificates. A budgerigar cannot become a champion bird exclusively in breeder classes. Once the necessary certificates have been accumulated, they are sent to the Budgerigar Society office for verification and a *champion bird certificate* is then issued. It has become the custom for birds achieving this honour to be given names as well as their numbers.

CHICKWEED
No other greenfood seems to be more enjoyed by budgerigars than chickweed. The plant should be gathered when fresh and care taken that it is not growing in a position where it could be fouled by petrol fumes or animal excrement, or sprayed with weedkiller.

Chickweed, like all other forms of greenfood, should not be gathered if it has been affected by frost. It should be washed and given to the birds while still wet, because they delight in rolling in it in this state. Any which is not eaten at the end of each day should be removed because it goes bad if left overnight and could cause diarrhoea. (See also *GREENFOOD*.)

CHLAMYDIA
This disease, also known as *psittacosis*, is rare in budgerigars, but it is also the only disease suffered by these birds which can be transmitted to man. It manifests itself as a chest and respiratory disease, usually with enteritis, slimy droppings and runny eyes in the birds. It is a serious disease, but it can be cured. In man, *Chlamydia psittaci* can cause anything from a mild cold to serious, prolonged, feverish chest disease, sore throats and severe headaches, and in man it is also contagious. It can be very serious in small children. Any breeder who suspects that any of his birds are suffering from chlamydia should contact Johnson Biologicals, Former Anatomy Building, Brownlow Street, University of Liverpool, L69 3BX, where expert advice can be obtained. A breeder who suspects that he, or a member of his family, could have contracted psittacosis, should tell a doctor the circumstances immediately.

CHOOSING YOUR PET
Two things are vital when choosing your pet budgerigar. It must be healthy and it must be young. The eyes should be bright, it should stand alert, there should be no sign of green or wetness around the vent, there should be no watery discharge from the nose. To decide whether the budgie is young or not, refer to the entry under *AGE*. It cannot be stressed too strongly that the bird should be under four months old if it is to make the perfect pet which will learn to talk and become completely tame. Colour is a matter of individual choice. There is a huge range from which to choose and most breeders, even if they do not

breed the variety or colour you desire themselves, can usually introduce you to someone else who does. It has often been said that cocks are more likely to talk than hens, but this is a fallacy. Budgies learn to talk by mimicry and the more they are spoken to, the more they learn to mimic. It is true, however, that cock birds usually have more friendly temperaments than hens, but provided one gains their confidence, hens can be very affectionate. Cocks have a blue *cere* (the band above the beak), whilst in the hen this is brown. However, as babies the cere is not fully developed and it is often difficult to distinguish between the two. It is advised that, where possible, the pet buyer who is not buying from an experienced breeder, should be accompanied by one.

CHROMOSOMES

A chromosome is the nucleus of the cell, and the cell is the unit of life. In each cell in its body the budgerigar has thirteen pairs of large chromosomes and a number, which it has been impossible to ascertain, of smaller chromosomes. These carry the genes which determine the bird's colour, size, size of spots, shape and every other characteristic. All the chromosomes appear in pairs except the sex chromosome. The cock has two of these, while the hen has only one X, or sex, chromosome and one smaller one which is designated as Y. This difference is very important and will be discussed in detail under *SEX LINKAGE*.

CINNAMON FACTOR

The cinnamon factor is one of the mutations which has appeared in budgerigars over the years. It is sex-linked, that is it cannot be carried in a hidden form by the hen. The effect of this factor is to change all the black feathers into cinnamon brown and to soften the main body colour.

CLASSIFICATION

It is important to read the classification in show schedules because they can differ from show to show. In almost every case there are separate classes scheduled for *any age* and *breeder* birds. These must be observed carefully as at most shows it is an offence to enter any age birds in the breeder classes, or to enter a bird in breeder classes which is not wearing the closed coded ring of the exhibitor. It is also important that you check that the *class number* you use from the classification is for the correct status under which you wish to show, because once you have exhibited under a higher status, it is not possible to revert to a lower one unless there are no classes scheduled for your status (in this case it is allowable to show in the next higher status without affecting future shows). For example, if the schedule shows only novice classes, it is permissible for a beginner to enter in novice classes for that show and then to revert to his own status at any later shows. Breeder classes are sometimes referred to as current year classes. In some countries no bird may be shown in any class unless it was bred by the owner.

CLEARFLIGHT

A mutation which appears to be related to the *pied variety*, the clearflight, as its name implies, has

A typical show classification.

Lancashire, Cheshire & North Wales B.S. (inc. I.O.M.).

ANY AGE CLASSES Champ.	Int.	Nov.	Beg.	CLASSIFICATION	BREEDERS CLASSES Champ.	Int.	Nov.	Beg.
1	71	141	211	Light Dark or Olive Green Cock				
2	72	142	212	Light Dark or Olive Green Hen				
3	73	143	213	Sky Blue Cock	36	106	176	246
4	74	144	214	Cobalt, Mauve or Violet Cock	37	107	177	247
5	75	145	215	Sky, Cobalt, Mauve or Violet Hen	38	108	178	248
6	76	146	216	Grey Cock	39	109	179	249
7	77	147	217	Grey Hen	40	110	180	250
8	78	148	218	Grey Green Cock	41	111	181	251
9	79	149	219	Grey Green Hen	42	112	182	252
10	80	150	220	Opaline Green incl. Opaline Grey Green Cock	43	113	183	253
11	81	151	221	Opaline Green incl. Opaline Grey Green Hen	44	114	184	254
12	82	152	222	Opaline Blue incl. Opaline Grey Cock	45	115	185	255
13	83	153	223	Opaline Blue incl. Opaline Grey Hen	46	116	186	256
14	84	154	224	Normal Cinnamon Cock	47	117	187	257
15	85	155	225	Normal Cinnamon Hen	48	118	188	258
16	86	156	226	Opaline Cinnamon Cock	49	119	189	259
17	87	157	227	Opaline Cinnamon Hen	50	120	190	260
18	88	158	228	Lutino Cock	51	121	191	261
19	89	159	229	Lutino Hen	52	122	192	262
20	90	160	230	Albino Cock	53	123	193	263
21	91	161	231	Albino Hen	54	124	194	264
					55	125	195	265
					56	126	196	266
22	92	162	232	Yellow-wing Cock				
23	93	163	233	Yellow-wing Hen				
24	94	164	234	White-wing Cock				
25	95	165	235	White-wing Hen	57	127	197	267
26	96	166	236	Dominant Pied or Clearflight Cock	58	128	198	268
27	97	167	237	Dominant Pied or Clearflight Hen	59	129	199	269
28	98	168	238	Rec. Pied inc. Dark Eyed Clear Cock	60	130	200	270
29	99	169	239	Rec. Pied inc. Dark Eyed Clear Hen	61	131	201	271
30	100	170	240	Any Colour or Variety Crested Cock	62	132	202	272
31	101	171	241	Any Colour or Variety Crested Hen	63	133	203	273
32	102	172	242	Yellow Face Cock	64	134	204	274
33	103	173	243	Yellow Face Hen	65	135	205	275
34	104	174	244	A.O.C. Cock	66	136	206	276
35	105	175	245	A.O.C. Hen	67	137	207	277
Any Age					68	138	208	278
281					69	139	209	279
282					70	140	210	280

JUNIOR CLASSES

281	Any Colour Normal Cock
282	Any Colour Normal Hen
283	Any Colour Opaline Cock
284	Any Colour Opaline Hen
285	Any Colour Normal or Opaline Cinnamon Cock
286	Any Colour Normal or Opaline Cinnamon Hen
287	Any Other Colour Cock
288	Any Other Colour Hen

Breeders

289
290
291
292
293
294
295
296

TEAM CLASS — Class No. 297 Team Class (4 Birds).
PET CLASS — Class No. 298 Pet Class (Sunday only).

Don't forget your Sales Classes — P.T.O.

Breeders Classes — All Birds competing in these classes must be wearing the closed coded rings of the actual exhibitor with the year 1987 thereon, such rings to have been purchased from the Budgerigar Society through the General Secretary. All entries MUST be accompanied by a written declaration on entry form to the effect that these conditions are in order.

visible flight feathers of clear yellow or white on its wings, according to the basic colour. The correct number for show purposes is seven. It also has a small patch of clear colour at the back of the head.

CLEARWINGS

First bred in 1933 in Australia, this mutation of budgerigars was much sought after when they were introduced into the UK a year later. However, when it was found that they were much smaller than the normal variety and that, because they were recessive to normals, it was difficult to improve the size, they became less popular with exhibitors. In good specimens the body colour is enhanced from that of the normal varieties and the wings are of a clear colour, lacking the *melanin markings*.

CLOSED CODED RINGS

These rings are supplied only by the Budgerigar Society in the United Kingdom, by the American BS in the United States and by the ruling body for the hobby in other countries. They are made from aluminium which has been dyed to a specific colour. The colour changes

Closed coded rings.

each year. On the ring is stamped the year, the individual code number of the breeder and then the serial number of the ring, for example, 87 (year), M1574 (code number), 107 (serial number). The rings are placed on the legs of the chicks at between five and ten days of age. Once the bones have hardened, it is impossible to remove the rings except by cutting them off.

CLUTCH

A number of eggs laid by the hen of

This clutch of eggs indicates the variation in size and shape that is possible in budgerigar eggs.

a breeding pair is called the clutch. In the wild, in Australia, a clutch of eggs is usually four, all of which hatch. In captivity the number ranges on average from three to nine and, unfortunately, a number fail to hatch. Some are *clear* or *infertile*, others die before they have started to form into chicks and are said to be *addled*, others begin to form into baby budgerigars and then die along the way; these are designated *dead-in-shell*, and then there are those which develop right up until the time of hatching, but lack the strength to break out of their shells.

The eggs are laid every other day and hatch in the same order, so that in a large clutch which all hatch successfully, it is possible to have one chick just a day old while the oldest is two weeks old. This causes problems with the big brother trampling all over the tiny baby, and the hen having run out of crop milk by the time the youngest is born. To prevent this situation, the older chicks are usually transferred to a nest containing chicks of roughly the same age, leaving the mother to bring up the smaller babies.

COD LIVER OIL

Cod liver oil emulsion is widely used to mix with canary seed during the breeding season. Some people feel that this could be the cause of *French moult*, but none of the research into the disease has served to confirm this belief. Experience has shown that the addition of a *small* amount of emulsion is beneficial to breeding hens and prevents *egg binding*, but this should not be given in excess. The amount recommended is one tablespoon to a 9 litre (2 gal) bucket of canary seed, well mixed in. Emulsion is preferable to plain oil, as it keeps better. Only sufficient for a week's supply should be mixed at a time, and in hot climates smaller amounts should be mixed, to ensure that the oil is never allowed to become rancid.

COLONY SYSTEM

The colony system of breeding is not one to be recommended. The theory is to keep an even number of cocks and hens together and then to supply them with far more nest boxes than there are pairs. Even when this precaution is taken, there are often fights among the hens for one particular nest box and these can be quite serious, in fact they have been known to fight to the death. If the reader should wish to follow this system, then the nest boxes should be positioned high up, near the roof and should not be supplied until the weather has become warm in spring. Always supply at least a third more nest boxes than there are pairs. Within a week you should see pairs going in and out of the nest boxes, around 18 to 21 days later the chicks should be hatching, and after a further 30 to 40 days the youngsters should be flying around the flight. Remember that certain colours are dominant and if you start with some greens among the flock, then eventually green will take over. The same thing happens with greys. They are a dominant variety and soon there will be more and more greys and grey greens and fewer and fewer blues.

Remember that when colony breeding is practised, the aviary can soon become overcrowded with birds, and unless all nest boxes are removed, the birds will keep on breeding, with chicks starting to hatch every ten weeks. Remember to remove *all* the nest boxes once the chicks have started to fly; this prevents quarrelling amongst the hens.

COLOURS

The range of colours and varieties of budgerigars becomes a source of amazement for the uninitiated. From the first wild normal light greens have mutated and evolved yellows, blues, pieds, clearwings, spangles, lutinos and a range which gives a wide choice to those seeking a pet or a variety upon which to concentrate when breeding.

COLOUR STANDARDS

These standards are set by the Budgerigar Society in the UK and are also used by several other countries as their standards. They consist of a minute description of the correct colour of wings, cheek patches, eyes, tail etc., of all the colours and varieties.

CONDITION

Condition is a term used to describe fitness for a desired goal. A budgerigar is in *show condition* when it has its complete set of feathers and those feathers are well groomed and have a bloom of good health. The eye is bright, the stance is upright, the vent is clean and the bird alert. It is in *breeding condition* when it has no sign of illness (wet or stained vent, discharge from eyes or nose, breathing difficulties, etc.), is alert and active, is tapping at the perches and, if housed together, is paying a great deal of attention to the opposite sex. It's not necessary for the birds' feathers to be perfect for them to be in breeding condition.

CONDITION SEED

This is a mixture of seeds which acts as a tonic to the birds and is generally greatly enjoyed. It is usually purchased ready-mixed from a seed merchant. Condition seed should only be given as an extra, and rationed accordingly, otherwise some birds might try to live exclusively on their favourite seeds which can have unfortunate results, particularly as one food which is often a favourite is hemp seed which has an intoxicating effect.

CREST

All colours of budgerigars can be shown under the crest classification. They are distinguished by a number

A budgerigar with a full-circular crest.

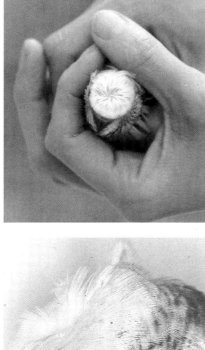

D

DARK FACTOR

The addition of two dark factors to the basic colours has led to some confusion in the names of the colours. A green bird carrying two dark factors is called an olive green, while if it carries only one dark factor it is referred to as a dark green. Similarly, with the blue colours, one dark factor results in a cobalt bird and two dark factors produce a mauve.

DEAD IN SHELL

When a chick is termed dead in shell, it means that it has developed for ten days or more and then, for some reason, died before it was hatched. Sometimes the reasons for this can be discovered by the fancier. It could be that the hen was uncomfortable and spent long periods away from the nest box. Perhaps the cock was disturbing the hen, or not supplying sufficient food and she came off the eggs to feed — and stayed away too long. In many instances the breeder himself is to blame, by continually disturbing the hen as he looks in the nest box, or shows the eggs to visitors to the birdroom. Infection can be another cause. Bacteria can be introduced from the hands of the breeder, or from droppings in the nest box, and can permeate the porous shell of the egg.

In some cases, the chick remains alive until it actually begins to chip its way out of the shell and then dies before it is clear. Sometimes this is a case of the chick being too weak to achieve its freedom from the confines of the egg, and in this case it would probably not survive into adulthood even if it were assisted, but in some instances the inside membrane of the shell has become over-dry and tough and in this case the hen may help by prising apart the two halves of the shell herself. The breeder may wish to attempt this himself, but must be very careful not to injure the tiny chick.

of feathers on the head growing in a different direction from the others, causing one of the three types of crests to appear. The *plain crest*, or *tuft*, consists of just a few feathers standing more or less upright in the centre of the head; the *half-circular crest* is a semi-circle of feathers rising or falling in a fringe just above the cere; the *full-circular crest* is flat, with the feathers radiating from the centre and falling all around the head in a circular fringe.

CUTTLEFISH

Cuttlefish bone, which is readily available from seed merchants and pet stores, is a vital source of calcium for the birds. It is beneficial to make it available at all times of the year, but during the breeding season it is absolutely essential, so that the hens are provided with a source of calcium from which to lay down supplies in the shell gland for the shells of their eggs.

DIET
The basic diet of the budgerigar is canary and millet seed, with the addition of essential vitamins and minerals. The subject is dealt with fully under *FEEDING*.

DISEASES see *AILMENTS*

DISINFECTANTS
It has been said that the finest disinfectant of all is strong bright sunlight after all debris has been removed by plenty of hot soap and water. However, as we cannot rely on strong sunlight just when we need it, and certainly cannot bring it inside our birdrooms, we need to use something really strong with which to remove all traces of bacteria or mite. The strongest, and most effective, disinfectant is one which is chlorous-based but, unfortunately, this is not one of the safest and if it is used where birds will have access to the surfaces treated, it should be well rinsed off with water. The simplest of these chlorous-based disinfectants is old-fashioned washing soda, but there are many proprietary brands on the market. One of the safest disinfectants for use on utensils and surfaces to which the birds have access is one with an iodine base, such as Vanodine, which is widely advertised in the bird press.

At the end of the breeding season, all the wire netting in the inside and outside flights should be washed down with a strong solution of iodine-based disinfectant and allowed to dry before the birds are reintroduced. All food and water containers must be removed before any disinfectants are used. The floor and walls of the outside flights should be really soaked with a strong chlorous-based disinfectant and later sprayed to rinse off any residue. Nest boxes and perches should be removed from the breeding cages, the fronts taken off, and emptied of whatever litter is used, scraped, brushed and then scrubbed with the iodine-based solution. Finally, the nest boxes, their blocks and the perches are scraped, brushed and soaked in a strong solution of disinfectant, liquid soap and paraffin. They are then scrubbed well and left in the sun to dry. Before they are stored away for the next season, a sprinkling of carbolic powder inside will ensure that they are kept mite-, lice- and bacteria-free. Before the cage fronts are put back, any necessary painting should be done and the cages sprayed with an anti-mite spray or water containing a solution of mite killer and repellant.

The most important thing to remember when carrying out the disinfection of your birdroom is that no food or water should have been left in a position where it could be contaminated by the disinfectants being used, and that the birds are removed from whichever part of the aviary you are cleaning.

DOMINANT FACTORS
Certain factors are dominant to others, which means that if you introduce these into your stock and breed indiscriminately, the factor which is dominant will eventually take over. Grey is a dominant factor and is visible in the green series as a modifying agent which changes the colour of green to grey green; in the blue series it masks the blue colour completely and results in an all grey bird. Other dominant factors are the green series, the Australian pied and violet, with a possibility of the spangle variety also being dominant.

DRAUGHTS
Human beings find draughts uncomfortable, but for a budgerigar they are fatal. Although they can withstand cold, will play in the snow and seem to enjoy flying around in windy weather, they cannot stand draughts. They will sit in a draught without moving away and very quickly become ill. When building a birdroom it is very important to ensure that the perches are fixed so that no draughts can occur in that area. With a little thought, good ventilation can be achieved without the birds having to suffer draughts.

Another way that birds can be placed in a draughty position is when travelling to or from a show. Car windows may be left slightly open, or the car ventilation system left on, with a cage near one of the outlets. Care should be taken to ensure that this does not happen, or a light cover placed over the show cages so that no draughts can enter. Covering the cages being transported to a show also has the advantage of keeping out flashing lights from passing cars or from street lighting which could disturb or frighten the birds.

A pet cage should never be hung where it might be in a draught from an open window or door. Again, if open doors or windows are necessary, the cage should be protected by a cloth cover thrown over the side open to the draught. This should be held securely with clothes pegs or something similar to make sure that the playful budgie does not push it away from inside the cage.

DRINKERS
For pet cages, the most sensible drinker is the fountain type. It clips onto the cage, the level of water is

Various types of drinkers, on the right is a fountain type of drinker which can be clipped on to a cage.

always visible and the bird cannot splash the water around or try to use it as a bath. For birdrooms and aviaries, various types are described under *WATER*. (See also *AUTOMATIC WATERING SYSTEM*.)

E

EGG BINDING
Lack of calcium can be one cause of egg binding. Sometimes the hen does not have sufficient supplies of this mineral to lay down around the yolk of the egg to make the shell, which results in the shell being malleable. The hen struggles to eject the egg which, being soft, elongates itself. This sort of straining can cause permanent damage to the hen and should be avoided at all costs. A supply of calcium must be always available. Oystershell and limestone grits are soluble forms of calcium, and cuttlefish, which is an integral part of the breeding cage furniture, is another valuable source.

Sometimes a hen has been put down to breed before being sufficiently mature and has trouble passing the egg through muscles which are not fully formed.

A diet containing plenty of greenstuff (provided that greenstuff has been given regularly in the past) and mixed seeds — with the canary seed treated with a small quantity of cod liver oil emulsion — is usually sufficient to prevent egg binding. Most causes of egg binding could and should be avoided.

If a hen does become egg bound, she should be moved, very gently to avoid breaking the egg inside her, to a show cage which can be placed before a hot fire or on a central heating radiator. Before a bird in a cage is left before an open fire for any reason, place a hand in front of the cage and leave it there to test the heat. Only when the heat is comfortable to the back of your hand should the cage be left unattended. It is unkind to leave a bird in a position where the heat is too great; it causes the bird great distress and it can soon become dehydrated. If a thermometer is available, the ideal temperature is 27° C (80° F). Now, with a feather or a very soft brush, the vent of the egg-bound hen should be coated

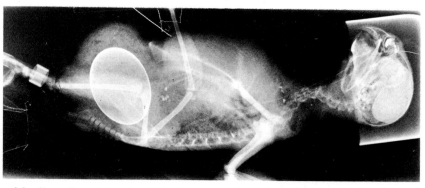

This x-ray shows a hen with a fully-formed egg about to be laid. Notice how large the egg is in proportion to the size of the bird.

with olive oil and she should be kept warm until she has expelled the egg.

EGG PRODUCTION
When the female *germ cell*, or *blastodisc*, falls into the *oviduct*, hopefully, a male *spermatazoa* will be waiting to fertilize it. A little further down the oviduct it is sheathed in *albumen*; even further along its journey, the membranes are formed and finally it reaches the *shell gland* where the hen has laid down stocks of calcium in readiness to make the shell. Once this is achieved, the egg is complete and after a short period needed for the egg to harden, it is laid.

EQUIPMENT
Much of the equipment used in a birdroom can be made at home. A very successful *food tray* can be made by using a length of PVC drainpipe with a table attached to the top. The table needs a 5 cm (2 in) surround to prevent food falling to the ground where it could attract vermin. The use of a smooth section of pipe as a pedestal also prevents mice gaining access to the food. It is best to have glass or metal hoppers on the table to prevent fouling by the birds' droppings. Another base for the tray could be two plastic buckets.

Yet another feeding method is to make a box and place a rigid wire tray inside it about 5-7.5 cm (2-3 in) from the top. The seed dishes are then placed on the wire grid and all the husks, grit and debris fall into the box to be emptied away.

Always remember to place the feeding trays at a low level, because flying upwards helps birds to develop muscles.

A perfect method of *soaking seed* can be made from two ordinary PVC buckets. A 7.5 litre (2 gal) bucket is drilled with several hundred tiny holes, around 3 mm (⅛ in) diameter. Oats or mung beans are placed in this and it is then placed inside an 11 litre (3 gal) bucket. The outside bucket is filled with water. The contents of the smaller bucket can then be washed through with ease

and when the seed is ready to be given to the birds, all that is necessary is to lift out the smaller bucket and swing it around two or three times to remove excess water.

A *rotating swing* is very easy to make from four pieces of 5 x 2.5 cm (2 x 1 in) timber. Make them into two Xs, and then take four pieces of 2 cm (¾ in) hardwood dowelling and fix them between the two end crosses. Fix a screw at the centre of each end and suspend the swing from the roof of the outside flight (see page 60).

One useful item of equipment,

A bucket drilled with numerous holes to allow water to drain away into a larger bucket in which it stands. It is used to soak oats, mung beans and other foodstuffs.

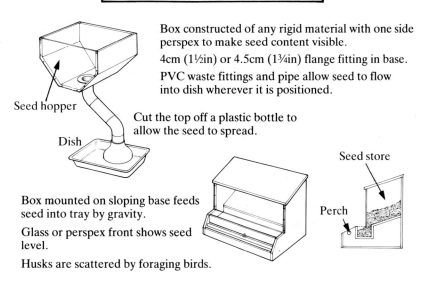

Box constructed of any rigid material with one side perspex to make seed content visible.

4cm (1½in) or 4.5cm (1¾in) flange fitting in base.

PVC waste fittings and pipe allow seed to flow into dish wherever it is positioned.

Seed hopper

Dish

Cut the top off a plastic bottle to allow the seed to spread.

Box mounted on sloping base feeds seed into tray by gravity.

Glass or perspex front shows seed level.

Husks are scattered by foraging birds.

Seed store

Perch

which cannot be made at home, is an *air cleaner*. These were made originally for cleaning the dust from calf houses, but are ideal for taking away the considerable amount of dust formed by the birds continually picking off minute pieces of their feather quills. The air cleaner works on the principle of sucking air into its interior which is filled with electrically charged plates. Any dust in the air is deposited on these plates before the air is expelled again. It is necessary to take out the plates and wash them occasionally. The amount of dust collected is very considerable.

Another useful item is an *electronic insect exterminator*. This unit emits ultra violet light which attracts most species of flying insects. They fly into the bars and the moment they touch these they are incinerated. These are often seen in butchers' shops, but are very efficient in keeping the birdroom free from flying creatures of all kinds, including moths which seem to congregate in seed and nest boxes. The dead insects fall into a tray which is easily emptied. The unit is very cheap to run. A wire guard must be fitted over it to prevent a bird which has become loose from flying into it.

A *humidifier* and *humidistat* are used in many birdrooms although their efficacy is often challenged. Their advocates feel that a humidity of 15° C (60° F) is vital to the hatchability of eggs, but others feel that the humidity of the birdroom has little effect on the hatching rate of eggs and that this is controlled by the micro climate around the egg itself. Many things can affect the humidity underneath the hen. Some sawdusts have a drying effect; some of the peats, if used damp, can create a humidity which will cause the egg to drown the forming chick. All materials appear to have their advantages and disadvantages, but since the most popular nest materials are sawdust and wood shavings, it would appear that these are giving the best results.

Turning to very sophisticated equipment, an item which can prevent worry for the breeder who is away from home during the day and unable to visit his birds until the evening, is a *photo-electric cell* fitted to the outside of the birdroom. If there is a thunder storm, or for any other reason the light dips below a certain point, the main lights of the birdroom come on and the birds are undisturbed by the storm. When the light returns to a level above the cut-off point, the lights are turned off automatically.

The humble clothes peg has so many uses. It can be used for holding greenfood, millet sprays, cuttlefish, pet cage covers or nest box record cards, to name but a few.

Another small item with a hundred uses is a 'Pop-On'. This is a clip made from wire springs, advertised in the fancy press, which will fasten almost anything.

EXHIBITING

Exhibiting is the life-blood of the budgerigar fancy. Although a few breeders are content to breed the little birds just for the love of their quaint antics and wonderful range of colours, the vast majority are drawn into the competitive world of bird shows, all certain that they have the dedication and knowledge necessary to reach the heights. At the outset, in the beginner section, in their own small club, they start to win rosettes and awards. It is this which causes many to 'get bitten by the budgie bug', as it is known in the fancy, and many years of competitive exhibiting, with the camaraderie, travelling and excitement which this entails will follow. There are a number of rules to be complied with when exhibiting, which are given under separate headings.

Very few shows schedule classes for pet birds but the annual national exhibition of cage and aviary birds does have a class for the best talking bird.

EYES

A budgerigar's eyes should be bright and alert. If there is any sign of a discharge from the eyes, or if they are dull and lifeless, it is a sure sign that all is not well. The bird should be caged separately, kept warm and observed until the reason for its condition is discovered. Any proprietary eye wash for human use can be used to treat the eyes of birds which are red and sore after a seed husk has been caught beneath the lids, or after the bird has been in a draught. The budgerigar should be held on its side and one or two drops of the eye wash dropped into the eye from an eye dropper, or squeezed from a piece of cotton wool soaked in the eye wash.

F

FALLOWS

The fallow factor dilutes the colour of the normal budgerigar to a much paler shade. The English fallows have bright red eyes, without an iris ring, while the German fallows have eyes of a deeper red, with the typical white iris ring of the normals.

FANCY

The budgerigar fancy is the name given to the hobby of breeding and exhibiting budgerigars. The UK parent body is the Budgerigar Society. Affiliated to the BS are ten area societies which accept the rules formulated by the parent body. They have the responsibility of administering and leading the hobby in their respective areas. They, in turn, have most of the small local societies affiliated to them, who also accept the ruling of the parent body. It is to one of these local societies that the newcomer to the fancy is attracted. They hold frequent meetings where speakers from the area society or Budgerigar Society share their knowledge, and they hold many small members' shows where beginners can learn about the art of exhibiting. The newcomers very soon join either their area society, or the Budgerigar Society, to enable them to obtain *closed coded rings*. Birds not wearing these rings cannot compete in breeder classes. Area societies usually produce journals or newsletters and offer their own patronage to their members and affiliated clubs.

Most serious breeders finally join the Budgerigar Society which is regarded by most of the world as the leader in matters concerning the budgerigar. Members are allocated a ring number which is exclusive to them for their life in the budgerigar fancy, a membership list which enables them to visit other members both in Great Britain and overseas, a handbook giving all the rules and descriptions of the various varieties of budgerigars, the standard of excellence for which they should aim, descriptions of standard show cages, all the information they will need in their career in the fancy and a free colour magazine every other month.

Another type of society is one catering for interest in one specific colour or variety of budgerigar. These societies are also affiliated to the Budgerigar Society and usually hold their shows in conjunction with the Budgerigar Society's world championship. There are specialist societies for *clearwings, lutinos* and *albinos, crests, rare varieties* and *colours* and for *variegated* budgerigars.

FAULTS

Judges discard or penalise birds showing any of the major faults. Some of these faults relate only to the variety being judged, such as *lutinos* showing a green suffusion, or *albinos* showing blue; some relate to most of the varieties, for example, flecking of *melanin* on the top of the head, a tail which droops down at an angle, or crossed wing tips. The aim is to breed a bird as near as possible to the standard which is considered ideal by the ruling body for the country in which the show is being held. Most of the faults are uniform world-wide.

FEATHERS

As far as the bird is concerned, the feathers perform three functions: they help it to fly, they help it to retain heat and they are a barrier against moisture. The serious exhibitor studies the density of the feathers, their length and texture. The budgerigar with coarse, or buff feathers will look larger than its fine, or yellow-feathered companions. A spot carried on a short feather will give the impression of a narrow mask, while a spot of equal size on a long feather will appear much lower down the mask. The keen exhibitor will, however, have to take into consideration the fact that the long, coarse-feathered birds have proved less productive than their fine-feathered friends in the breeding cages.

Feathers can give an indication of the health of the bird. On a very hot summer's day, the bird will fluff out its feathers to allow every bit of air to reach the skin and so cool it down, but if this condition is noticed on a cold day, it is a sure indication that the bird has a high temperature and is trying to lose heat. In this case it should be caught, caged separately, kept warm, observed for any signs of illness and appropriate action taken. If the feathers on top of the head or around the beak are matted, it is a sign that the bird has been vomiting, or that there is a discharge from the beak and nostrils. Again, this is something which must be investigated.

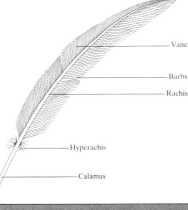

The structure of a budgerigar feather.

Vane

Barbs

Rachis

Hyperachis

Calamus

Feathers carrying spots of different shapes at different levels.

Budgerigars constantly *preen* their feathers to keep them in good condition and to 'rain-proof' them. They possess a preening gland at the base of the wings which produces a substance similar to lanolin with which they coat each feather. When the fancier sprays the bird's feathers regularly before a show, this removes a tiny amount of the lanolin and so encourages the bird to preen and keep its feathers in perfect order. If a bird is seen with lack-lustre, straggly feathers, it usually means that it is not preening which indicates that the bird may be unwell. The usual routine of catching and observing is necessary.

FEATHER DUSTERS

These unfortunate birds have been called the 'Down's syndrome' victims of the budgerigar world. During their early formation they appear the same as their normal brothers and sisters, but at the age of around four weeks, the growth of their feathers changes. There is more space between each follicle and the feathers begin to grow long and curled. Before long the chick appears to be much larger than its

A feather duster.

contemporaries, very often much larger than its parents. It continually loses the long feathers and then grows more of the same type. Most of its day is spent in searching for food and eating. Although not blind, it often seems unsure of where to find its food. If it is placed in the middle of a food dish it will eat ravenously, but soon lose its bearings and be found in another part of the cage. It is believed that the cause of this condition is hereditary, but no conclusive evidence of this has been found. The life span ranges from a few weeks to several months, but these birds seldom survive to adulthood.

FEATHER PLUCKING

Feather plucking is a most annoying habit and is difficult to stop. The hen is usually the culprit and often starts to pluck out the feathers of her babies simply out of the boredom of sitting in a nest box for a long period. It has been suggested that this habit is hereditary, or that a hen which has been plucked when she was a baby is likely to pluck her own chicks. If the hen simply pulls out the fine down and stops before the feathers begin to grow, little harm is done, but in some cases the hen will pull out the feathers themselves, sometimes drawing blood and causing the youngster a great deal of distress. In severe cases, the feathers never regrow and the bird is useless for show purposes even provided that it recovers from the hen's attack. There are a number of proprietary liquids available to paint or spray onto the chick, which should deter the hen, alternatively it can be plastered with a greasy face cream or petroleum jelly to make it too unpalatable to pluck. If nothing stops the hen from plucking, she should be removed and the cock left to rear the chicks.

FEEDING

Budgerigars need protein, fats, carbohydrates, vitamins and minerals to keep them in good health, but at different times of the year these are required in different proportions. As well as the climatic seasons, it is necessary to take into account the moulting season, the breeding season, the growing period of young birds and the show season.

During *the moult*, or *resting season*, feeding should be fairly basic. At this time of the year the birds are not very active and are not being worked up to show condition. They should be kept fit and healthy, but not made too active by the addition of tonic or conditioning seed. The diet should consist of canary seed to provide protein, mixed with cod liver oil emulsion which adds both fat and Vitamins A and D. The oil is mixed in by hand, at the rate of one tablespoonful to a 7.5 litre (2 gal) bucket of seed. Provided that the autumn is average and that no freak high temperatures are experienced, there is no likelihood of the oil becoming rancid. In a separate container a mixture of millets is offered, consisting of 70 per cent *pannicum*,

20 per cent *white* and 10 per cent *Japanese millet*. Both canary seed and millet seed are replenished as they are eaten. In the early days of the moult it is usual to find that the millets are the favourite food, but as the building phase of growing new feathers arrives, the intake of canary seed becomes very high. It appears that when offered a selection of seeds, the budgerigar chooses what is most likely to be of benefit.

In every season of the year, there must be a plentiful supply of *grit* available to supply the essential minerals and to help the bird to grind up its food. See entry under *GRIT*.

Millet sprays can be offered occasionally, just as a titbit. The budgies love to strip them and then spend endless hours playing with the stalks. They are particularly enjoyed by youngsters.

Greenfoods, especially chickweed, fruit or carrots are needed to supply the necessary vitamins. Make sure that greenfood offered has not been frosted or contaminated.

The breeding season places a greater demand upon the birds than any other time of the year. The hen must produce eggs and both cock and hen will feed the chicks. Some budgerigars are so enthusiastic about feeding their young that they can almost starve themselves. Food must always be freely available to them and extras at this season are highly recommended. The mixed millets and oil-treated canary seed should continue to be given in separate dishes. The recommended amount of oil added to the canary seed should be continued until the second round of eggs has been laid and then gradually reduced over a period of three weeks, after which the oil becomes unnecessary and the canary seed can be fed untreated. Although no research has been carried out into the subject, it has been frequently observed in the authors' birdroom that the pairs who regularly empty the canary-seed pot, eating very little millet, are those who produce a good number of *fertile eggs*, while the pairs which eat mostly mixed millets tend to have a number of *clear eggs* or all clear eggs in their clutches.

There is a definite cycle prior to and during egg laying and hatching. The intake of canary seed remains high until the first chick is ten to

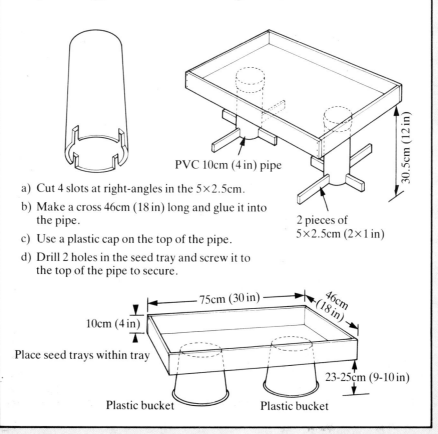

Two examples of home-made feeding trays grounded on a PVC pipe (top) and on plastic buckets (bottom). These reduce litter when placed inside aviaries.

PVC 10cm (4 in) pipe

a) Cut 4 slots at right-angles in the 5×2.5cm.
b) Make a cross 46cm (18 in) long and glue it into the pipe.
c) Use a plastic cap on the top of the pipe.
d) Drill 2 holes in the seed tray and screw it to the top of the pipe to secure.

2 pieces of 5×2.5cm (2×1 in)

30.5cm (12 in)

75cm (30 in)

46cm (18 in)

10cm (4 in)

Place seed trays within tray

23-25cm (9-10 in)

Plastic bucket   Plastic bucket

Cinnamon and opaline cinnamon

Cinnamon grey
cock

Opaline cinnamon
light green hen

A Capern's card
showing a
Cinnamon Grey
Budgerigar

Opaline cinnamon
grey green cock.
This bird shows the
perfect example of
the "powder puff"
head so much
desired by
exhibitors

fourteen days old and then decreases, with a higher intake of millets. When the chick is four to five weeks old and egg laying begins again, the pair switch back to their preference for canary seed.

Soaked oats are an additional food supply which the birds greatly enjoy and which can be fed three days prior to the time the first egg is due to hatch. The oats should be soaked for 24 to 30 hours and the water changed several times, particularly in hot weather. A bucket which facilitates the soaking of seed is described under *EQUIPMENT*. The soaked oats can be given straightaway, but within 48 hours both sprouts and roots will begin to grow and at this stage the birds will devour them with great enthusiasm. Two heaped teaspoonfuls of soaked oats is a reasonable daily ration for a pair and this can be doubled as the chicks hatch. Early morning is the best time to feed oats, so that they can be eaten during the day and none is left to go stale overnight. Once the chicks have been taken away, the oats can be discontinued for four to seven days. The chicks are given soaked oats until they are around sixteen weeks old, but

should then be gradually weaned off them by feeding them every other day, then perhaps twice a week. If they are given soaked oats for any longer than this, they are liable to form fat and become overweight. It is then difficult to get rid of this sort of bulk.

Another beneficial extra is *soaked mung beans*. They are soaked in the same way as the oats, for 24 to 30 hours, and are then kept in a warm place, such as an airing cupboard or next to a radiator, for a further twelve hours. They are not as universally popular with the birds as the oats, but once youngsters have had them as part of their diet from birth, they take to them readily. As they add essential vitamins to the diet, it is recommended that a small amount should be offered daily.

One word of caution with all soaked seeds. Always throw away any soaked seed which begins to smell sour or musty. It is far more important to keep the birds healthy and alive than to save a few handfuls of sour oats or mung beans.

A very nutritious softfood, which can be fed each evening in a finger drawer, can be made up in a food processor. Three average-sized raw

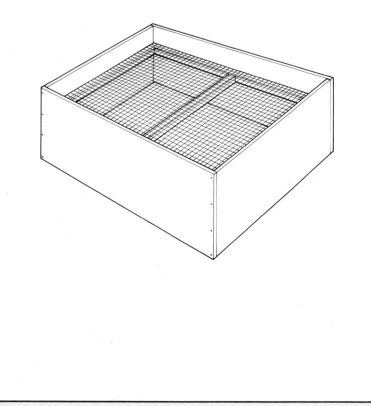

Diagram of a home-made feeding tray. Make a wooden box with ½in (1.25 cm) plywood 15in (38 cm) deep. Fit a batten 4in (10 cm) from the top all around the sides and across the centre as a stiffener. Place a piece of weldmesh inside the box and across the top of the battens. Now place the seed dishes on the wire and the husks will fall through the wire grill to be cleaned up later.

carrots are processed, four hard-boiled eggs, complete with shells, are added and processed for a few seconds, next three teacups of dry wholemeal breadcrumbs and four heaped teaspoons of powdered bee pollen are added and the whole processed for a few more seconds until it becomes a moist and crumbly mixture. This mixture contains almost every nutrient required by the breeding pairs. Bee pollen is nature's most perfect food, containing protein, trace minerals and vitamins including concentrated vitamin E, so vital to high fertility. It is wise to store this in a polythene container and keep it in a refrigerator. If only a small number of pairs are kept, then only half the above quantity should be made at one time.

Cuttlefish must always be available, together with a supply of grit which must be replenished regularly. It is a mistake to think that because there is still grit in a dish it is not necessary to change it. The birds are selective, picking out the kinds of grit they need at that particular time and so the dish must be refilled with mixed grits to allow them to choose. Another reason is that very often what they have left is far too fine to be of use to them.

During the *growing season* the youngsters need to be weaned from all the additives they have had in the breeding cages. Food needs to be more basic, but it must be freely available as it is important for the young birds to maintain their body weight as they grow. They should be given as much canary seed and mixed millet seed as they can eat, plus occasional millet sprays as a treat. About three times a week, dry oats should be given and will be much enjoyed. Softfood is not advisable at this time, but fresh greenfood and ripe fruit supply vitamins and are greatly welcomed. The grit dish should be watched and as soon as it becomes fine, it should be thrown away and replaced with a new supply.

During the *show season* the show team are usually kept in stock cages which limits the amount of flying they do. This could lead to them becoming overweight which spoils the outline of a show bird and frequently becomes permanent. To avoid this, the amount of mixed millets, which contain a high proportion of carbohydrates, should be restricted. Unlimited supplies of canary seed must be available. Whilst greenfood, fruit and carrot can be offered, exhibitors must be careful not to give these just before a show because they can badly stain the feathers and these stains are sometimes almost impossible to remove. As at any other season of the year, grit must be always provided.

When the birds return from a show, a millet spray and some dry oats will be eagerly devoured and will ensure that the birds are well fed before settling down for the night. This may mean extending the hours of artificial light for that evening, but it is wise to ensure that the birds have a good feed in familiar surroundings.

FERTILITY

Fertility is a growing problem among budgerigar breeders. The belief is that the desire for ever bigger and longer birds has led to a smaller number of eggs being fertilised. Another theory is that almost every top class show bird is related. Over the years, best has been bred to best and those youngsters which have not quite made the grade sold to the breeders a little further down the ladder until, eventually, almost every breeder is inadvertantly inbreeding. Whether this belief is true or not has not been proved, but the introduction, from Australia, of the new *spangle mutation* has undoubtedly introduced a new, hybrid vigour into the UK stock.

FINGER TRAINING

The breeder whose main object is to supply the pet market can, undoubtedly, obtain higher prices for his budgerigars if he, or some member of his family, will undertake the fairly simple and enjoyable task of finger training his birds. Tameness begins in the nest box, and the more chicks are handled at this stage, the sooner they lose any

The ino varieties

A lutino hen with a
good deep golden
colour

Two Capern's cards
showing a Lutino
and a Cobalt

Albino hen

The Australian contrast

Two Australian clearwings, one yellowwing dark green hen and one yellowwing olive hen. The bird on the right appears to be losing a little of the "Australian" contrast.

Two Australian whitewing cobalt hens with brilliant contrast between the white wings and the deep body colour

Budgerigars will treat a finger as another perch if trained properly.

fear of the human hand. Once they leave the nest box the breeder can encourage them to stand on his finger or hand by holding millet sprays, pieces of sweet apple, sprays of chickweed or other treats in his hand. When the youngsters are ready to leave their parents and feed independently, it is a good plan to keep them in a normal pet cage to get them used to the sort of environment in which they will be living permanently. If the habit of feeding treats by hand has been followed, it will be found that as a finger is put into the cage, the baby budgies will automatically jump onto it, looking for special treats.

The owner of a new pet which has not been finger trained has a slightly more difficult task, as the youngster's natural nervousness has to be overcome. The owner should stand close to the cage and talk to the bird as often as possible to gain its confidence. Once it has lost its first nervousness, it will allow the owner to scratch its head. This is an act which budgies seem to enjoy a great deal. This is probably because they can pick at almost any other part of their bodies themselves, but they have to rely on their companions to scratch and pick the top of their heads. In an aviary, this

head picking can be seen, with one bird turning and twisting its head for another to scratch every portion. When the bird has learned that fingers seem to be friendly items, which are beneficial rather than fearsome, open the cage and put in a finger, and later the hand. It is important to cover up the opening with the other hand in case the bird tries to fly away. Once the bird has accepted that hands don't hurt and are no menace, the same procedure of offering treats should be followed. When a baby bird realises that the hand will do it no harm, it accepts the finger as an extension to its other perches and walks onto it quite fearlessly.

FLECKING

Flecking is a fault in exhibition budgerigars and is penalised by the judges. A bird is considered flecked if there are flecks of *melanin* or *striations* on the cap of the bird, which should be clear. This is also referred to as *ticking* or *frosting*, but whatever the name, the penalty is the same. This particular fault has caused more controversy over the years than any other. Many fanciers have called for a complete ban to be placed on the exhibition of these birds. At one time, no bird

Budgerigars
showing differing
degrees of flecking.

demonstrating flecking was allowed
to win a first prize. At the moment
the judges are left to decide the
degree of penalty which should be
awarded, according to the degree of
flecking in evidence. It is an offence
to try to bleach the black *melanin*
from these feathers, or to pluck
them out.

FLIGHTS

Ideally, the birdroom should have
inside and outside flights. For the
inside flight, a frame should be made
of 5 x 5 cm (2 x 2 in) timber with a
suitable sized door for you to gain
access to the flight, and it is well
worth including a small hinged door
for returning birds to the flight
without the need to open the main

door. This will prevent any birds
from flying out into the main
birdroom. If a solid panel is fitted
along the bottom of the flight, this
will prevent the husks blowing all
over the birdroom. The wooden
frame is painted and then covered
with strong wire netting, preferably
2 x 2 cm (¾ x ¾ in).

Windows need to be fitted,
leading to the outside flights. It is
important to position these so that
the maximum flying space is
available for the birds. It is also
important that they are positioned
so that the perches are high above
the tops of the windows. This
eliminates the fear of draughts and
reduces the chance of *night fright*
due to lights being switched on in a
nearby house or a car headlight
flashing across the birdroom.

The outside flight should be as
large as possible, to give the birds
plenty of flying space. Once the size
has been determined, a frame is
made of 5 x 5 cm (2 x 2 in) timber
or, in larger sizes, of 7.5 x 5 cm (3 x
2 in). Make it as strong as possible,
particularly in northern climates
where it may have to support the
weight of snow in winter. Before
fixing or fitting the weldmesh, give
the frame a good coating of non-
toxic wood preservative. Secure 2 x
2 cm (¾ x ¾ in) weldmesh to the
frame giving it two coats of black
bitumastic paint to protect the wire
against rust. Now secure the frame
well to the birdroom wall at one end
and fasten it securely to the ground
at the opposite end. It is advisable
to dig a trench, 30 cm (12 in) deep,
around the flight then fix some
heavy gauge 2.5 x 1.25 cm (1 x ½ in)
wire netting from the bottom of the
flight frame to the bottom of the
trench and then turning outwards,
away from the flight, for at least
another 23 cm (9 in). The trench
should then be filled with stone
chippings. This will deter any
vermin. The floor of the outside
flight is covered to a depth of 7.5-10
cm (3-4 in) with 2 cm (¾ in) stone
chippings. Again, this is to deter
vermin, but it also makes the floor
more hygienic, because droppings
will wash through. The dampness of
the chippings keeps alive grubs

Yellowface
cinnamon opaline
grey cock.

The yellowface variety

This Australian yellowface mauve hen illustrates the intensity of the yellow colour in the Australian birds.

Yellowface grey cock.

Yellowface opaline grey hen – note the lack of yellow pigment in the mask.

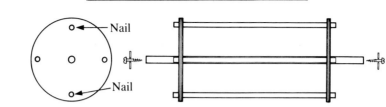

Two methods of making a rotating swing.

a) Cut 2 discs of 1.25cm (½ in) plywood 23cm (9 in) diameter.
b) Drill 4 holes that will take 1.5cm (⅝ in) diameter dowel.
c) Drill 2cm (¾ in) centre hole to take 1.5cm diameter dowel.
d) Cut 1 piece of 1.5cm (¾ in) dowel 61cm (24 in) long.
e) Cut 4 pieces 1.5cm (⅝ in) dowel 46cm (18 in) long.
f) Fit the 5 pieces of dowel by tapping them into place. Tap thin nails into 2 dowels to lock them into position.
g) Drill a 3mm (⅛ in) in the centre of the 1.5cm (¾ in) dowel at each end.
h) Place 2 penny washers on a 4cm (1½in) wood screw. Drive into the ends on the centre dowel.
i) Using 3mm (⅛ in) galvanised wires, hang the swing level from the roof of the outside flight.
j) Loosen the screws slightly until the swing rotates freely.

B. Alternative method
a) Cut 4 pieces of 5×2.5cm (2×1 in) 25cm (10 in) long and drill 2 holes (see b above).
b) Position 2 pieces as a cross and fix with pins.
c) Cut 4 pieces of 1.5cm (⅝ in) dowel (see e above).
d) Fit the 4 pieces of dowel (see f above).
e) Cut off the dowels flush on the outer sides.
f) Fit 2 screws (see h above) and then follow i and j above.

which the birds seem to enjoy. In a long dry spell, the chippings can be hosed down, clearing away any accumulated droppings as the water drains away.

Part of the roof should be covered to allow the birds to shelter from heavy rain or hot sun. As soon as it begins to rain, the birds can be seen congregating on the outside wires, enjoying the sensation of getting wet, but they know exactly how wet they want to be and fly to a sheltered area as soon as they have been in the rain long enough. They become very bedraggled and unhappy if they cannot escape from heavy rain.

One item which gives the birds endless pleasure, as well as good exercise, is a *rotating swing*. Instructions for making one of these are given above.

FLOOR COVERINGS
In a pet cage, the ideal floor covering is the sanded sheets sold for the purpose in all pet shops. Most cages have a sliding tray into which these sand sheets will fit. Some are perforated and are adaptable for any size cage, while others come in various sizes. They are stiff and hard and difficult to break up, which is an advantage when dealing with any of the birds with parrot-type beaks, because tearing things up is part of their recreation. The sheets are very hygienic because they are thrown away after use and all debris and droppings are thrown out with them. An economical floor covering is a sheet of heavy duty hard polythene cut to size. If this is used, it is as well to have two cut at the same time, then one can be taken out for cleaning and the second one substituted. They should be soaked to loosen the droppings, washed clean and immersed in disinfectant before being re-used. Finally, newspaper can be used but the aforesaid tearing habits often results in masses of tiny pieces of newspaper being scattered around the room when the bird flies.

In birdroom and aviary, different types of floor covering are suitable in different areas. Vinyl asbestos tiles or lino are the best covering for the main birdroom floor, because both are easy to clean with water, they can be very efficiently disinfected, and there are no cracks and crannies for old seed to accumulate and go mouldy, or for seed to fall through and make a feeding ground for vermin.

In the breeding cages, the breeders' personal choice comes into play. The authors recommend the deep litter system and provide a thick layer of sawdust or wood shavings. The wood shavings have the advantage of providing entertainment and relieving boredom, as the birds chew it up into a type of coarse sawdust. The deep litter system provides a soft cushion for the chicks to fall onto when they first come out of the nest box, and is not too unfamiliar from the nest box environment when the chicks come out and huddle together in a corner or behind the seed tray, half hidden in the shavings. Another covering which is used is newspapers, which can be frequently changed, but an endless supply is necessary. Or there are those breeders who prefer no deep litter and leave the floor as plain wood with no covering whatsoever.

The inside flights can have a plain concrete floor which needs scraping and scrubbing to clean it, or a thin layer of sawdust or shavings can be used so that droppings are more easily removed. Some find that the same covering as that of the main birdroom floor is very convenient, as far as cleaning is concerned, but if tiles or lino are used, they should be stuck down firmly and sealed at the edges, so that water does not get through, causing mouldy patches.

The floors of the outside flights can be of soil, which is dug over fairly frequently to prevent it becoming sour through the constant droppings, and to present a fresh layer containing various grubs for the birds: the disadvantage here is that rodents could easily burrow up through the soil. It can be of a deep layer of sand, but in this case the sand, if sea sand, should be well washed before use to clean out all the salt. Unfortunately sand washes away fairly quickly and needs frequent replenishing. The

recommended covering is large stone chippings which can be shovelled over and washed through with disinfectant, then rinsed with clear water to keep them clean and hygienic.

FRENCH MOULT
Much research has taken place into the possible cause of this disease and many theories have been propounded, but, as yet, neither cause nor cure has been discovered. One group of fanciers support the theory that the cause is some deficiency, or even excess, in the diet; others are convinced that a virus is the cause. Lack of protein, overdosage of vitamins, the inability of the hen to produce crop milk, even the presence of moths in the

French moult is an inexplicable condition, the cause of which is still unknown.

birdroom have all been blamed for outbreaks of the disease, and the number of 'cures' recommended are innumerable, but the disease remains as inexplicable as ever.

French moult usually becomes apparent in the nest box at any time after the feathers have begun to form. In severe cases, the feathers begin to drop when the chick is little over two weeks old: tiny, half-formed feathers will be noticed in the nest box and the poor chick continues to drop its feathers as soon as they grow, making it a pathetic, almost naked creature when it is ready to leave the nest box. Birds

Clearwings

A whitewing sky-blue budgerigar.

British whitewing cobalt cock which demonstrates how some of the colour contrast has been lost in the quest for size.

British yellow-wing dark green hen.

British whitewing skyblue cock.

A British
yellowface skyblue
cock.

Left: A yellow-
faced skyblue
budgerigar on a
Capern's card.

Far left: a
whitewing cobalt
budgerigar.

affected to this extent seldom recover and it is kinder to put them to sleep humanely. In milder cases, the chick begins to lose its feathers just before or just after it leaves the box. The flights and tail feathers are those most likely to be affected. These youngsers are unable to fly until they have regrown the feathers and should be kept in a stock cage, with water and seed available somewhere low enough for them to reach it, until they are able to fly with ease.

In yet another form of the disease, all the feathers grow normally, the youngsters leave the nest box fully fledged, and then, without warning, some, or all, of the flight and tail feathers suddenly drop off. As with the chicks described above, these birds, even if they have been allowed into the flights, should be returned to a stock cage to regrow their full complement of feathers.

FRONTAL RISE
This is a term used to describe the way in which a budgerigar is able to display the rise of its feathers from the top of the cere to the centre of its head. A tightly tucked-in beak with an exaggerated circle of feathers rising to the top of the head is greatly admired in show circles.

A superb cock budgerigar lifting its head feathers to display its frontal rise.

G

GENERAL COUNCIL
The general council of the Budgerigar Society is the governing body of the budgerigar fancy in Britain. The members formulate the rules under which shows are run, the general rules of the society and the standards for the many varieties of birds which are exhibited. There are 40 members; two are sent as delegates from each area society and the remaining twenty are chosen by ballot each year. All paid-up members are eligible to vote and are provided with a ballot form annually. The elected members serve a term of two years before re-election, therefore ten are elected in each year's ballot. Meetings of the general council are held twice yearly unless emergency meetings are required. The May meetings move from one area society to another each year, which means there will be ten different venues. This allows as many members as possible the opportunity of attending an annual general meeting. The meetings in October alternate between the north and south of the country. Sub-committees are chosen to administer finance, judges and colour standards, the world championship show and any other activity in which a sub-committee is considered appropriate.

GENES
Genes are units of inheritance. They affect every aspect of every person or animal. In budgerigars the genes about which we know most are those which affect colour. We know that if a bird is green, one of the parents was carrying a 'green gene'. What is not generally realised, and has not been studied in depth, as far as is known, is that everything – length of feather, size, size of spots, position of beak or eye – is carried in the genes of the bird. Perhaps one day, after much research, someone will be able to list the dominant and

recessive genes for all the desirable features of a show budgerigar, but at the moment it is very much a matter of trial and error, or sheer luck.

GENETICS

Genetics is the science of inheritance. It is a complex subject which deserves a book of its own and several excellent volumes on the subject are available. In budgerigars, the science of genetics is used, in the main, to forecast the expectations of colours or varieties. A large number of facts are accepted by even the newest beginner, but not so many understand the method by which the laws of colour inheritance work. The simplest method of learning about this subject is to make a chart using letters to indicate the colours. It is rare to find a pure bird which has not been mated with another colour and is, therefore, not carrying the other colour in a split form. However, let us imagine that we have a pure, unsplit green bird to mate to a pure unsplit blue. Let XX stand for a cock and XY for a hen, G for green and B for blue. A chart could be prepared as follows:

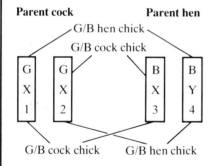

Each of the parents is carrying two potentials for colour. If we take potential number 1 from the cock, with potential number 3 from the hen, we produce a green youngster which is split for blue. As green is dominant to blue, the bird will be visibly green, but carrying a hidden (or split) potential for blue. Take potential number 2 from the cock, with number 4 from the hen, and you arrive at the same result, as would 1 and 4, or 2 and 3. It is impossible to breed from this pair anything but green birds carrying a blue split.

Now, if we mate together two of the split birds we have produced, the chart would read:

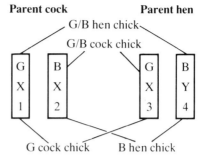

We take potential number 1 from the cock and number 3 from the hen, they are both green, they are both Xs, and so we have produced a green cock. If we take 1 from the cock with 4 from the hen, we have one G and one B, one X and one Y, which means we have bred a green/blue (visual green) hen. Take number 2 from the cock with number 3 from the hen and we have two Xs again, which means another cock, and this time a B and a G. Since green is dominant over blue, we would again have a visually green bird with a hidden blue potential. Finally, however, potential number 2 from the cock could tie up with number 4 from the hen, both Bs, and this would give us a pure blue hen.

Using this very simple method, giving each colour or variety a different initial, all the colour expectations can be worked out.

Unfortunately, other factors can complicate matters. The opaline factor, cinnamon, lutino, albino, lacewing and slate factors are all *sex-linked*, that is, the factor cannot be carried by the Y potential of the hen. The *opaline factor*, designated O, can be carried by either of the two Xs of the cock. A chart to prove this theory, based on two green/blue birds, the cock being a split opaline and the hen an opaline, would look like this:

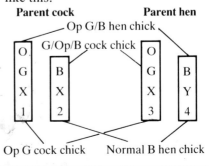

If we take 1 from the cock carrying the O factor, with 3 from the hen, we have OGX and OGX, or in other words an opaline green cock.

Potential number 2 from the cock, with number 3 from the hen, gives BX and OGX, a split opaline cock, but this time it is green/blue. Potential number 1 from the cock carrying the opaline potenttial, with 4 from the hen, would result in OGX and BY. The resulting chick would be a hen, it would be visibly green, but split for blue, *and it would be an opaline*. Whilst the cock needs two opaline factors for the opaline to be visible, a hen is a visible opaline if it has any opaline factor. If number 2 from the cock joined with number 4 from the hen, a non-opaline hen would be the result. The O factor, which is floating could also combine with potential number 2.

C for cinnamon could be substituted for the O for opaline and the same result would be achieved. In the same way expectations for lutino, albino, slate and lacewing can also be worked out.

For those who find the whole subject too perplexing, charts giving every possible mating have been worked out by Dr D. H. Duncker and are incorporated in the book *Budgerigar Matings and Colour Expectations*, published by the Budgerigar Society.

A table for cinnamons, which would apply to all sex-linked varieties is given below.

GREENFOOD

This is rather a loose term as various vegetables can be included under this description. Care must be taken when feeding any form of greenfood. It must be fresh, it must be uncontaminated by animals or garden sprays and it should be given regularly. It should not be given in excess and any left over at the end of a day must be removed.

Chickweed is the greenfood most enjoyed by budgerigars in the UK, particularly when it is in bud, as the buds are full of a nutritious milky sap. In Australia, and for that matter anywhere that the trees can be persuaded to grow, eucalyptus leaves are the greatest treat. Cabbage, spinach, lettuce, parsley, dandelion leaves, sweet apple, carrots and beetroot are all taken with enjoyment. Whilst budgerigars do not normally overeat, if large amounts are available, they will eat more greenfood than is good for them, resulting in diarrhoea, therefore the breeder must ration the supply. A small handful in the breeding cages is ample. In flights, bunches can be hung up or put on shelves, but the amounts should be limited.

It is better to give root vegetables in dishes to avoid them being dragged around the floor and possibly fouled with droppings.

SEX-LINKED VARIETIES

MATINGS		EXPECTATIONS	
Cock	**Hen**	**Cocks**	**Hens**
1 Cinnamon x Non-Cinnamon		Split Cinnamon	Cinnamon
2 Cinnamon x Cinnamon		Cinnamon	Cinnamon
3 Split Cinnamon x Non-Cinnamon		Split Cinnamon and Non-Cinnamon	Cinnamon and Non-Cinnamon
4 Split Cinnamon x Cinnamon		Cinnamon and Split Cinnamon	Cinnamon and Non-Cinnamon
5 Non-Cinnamon x Cinnamon		Split Cinnamon	Non-Cinnamon

Hens cannot be split for any sex-linked variety.

Most root vegetables are better fed grated. Greenfood can result in staining of the facial feathers and mask and so should not be given to birds just before a show. Whilst all greenfood left over must be removed in the evening so that it cannot putrify overnight and be consumed by the birds in that state in the morning, the stalks of cabbage or spinach can be left because they do not rot so quickly and the birds love to play with them. An excellent way to feed greenfood is to contact a firm supplying powdered grass. A heaped teaspoon of this added to the oil-treated canary seed can supply all the necessary vitamins to breeding pairs.

The vital rules again are: *not frosted, not contaminated, not stale and not a lot!* (See *CHICKWEED* and *GROUNDSEL.*)

GREY FACTOR
The grey factor is often misunderstood. Because a bird carrying two grey factors will always produce all grey progeny, it has been thought that grey is a new colour, but it is not. Every visual grey bird is a blue series bird which has been modified by one or two grey factors. If the bird is carrying the grey in a single factor, and is mated to a blue bird, the youngsters may be grey or blue, but if the grey bird is carrying two grey factors, then all the offspring will be visually grey but will be carrying only one grey factor. Equally, if the grey bird is mated with a green, then the grey factor will modify the green, turning it into grey green. The grey factor can be introduced into all the varieties and colours and will modify them all in the same manner: all the birds of the blue series will lose their original colour and appear grey, whilst the green series will change their original shade to a more muted shade with grey.

GRIT
Grit is essential to the budgerigar for the digestion of its food. One portion of the gizzard consists of two hardened pads especially designed for grinding together the seed and grit. Grit must therefore always be available to the birds who will know themselves how much they need and take it accordingly. Unfortunately, the birds are both playful and naturally destructive and will reduce the grit into a fine dust within a short time, so that it is necessary to inspect the grit dishes regularly, throw away the fine dust and replenish with a coarser grit. A good mixture can be made from oyster shell, limestone, mineral grit, large pigeon grit and large grains of sea-sand from a clean beach which have been washed clean of salt.

GROUNDSEL
This is a weed which is enjoyed by most budgies, but, as with all other kinds of greenfood, care must be taken to see that it has not been

A sprig of groundsel.

contaminated. If there is any likelihood that cats or other pets could have sprayed it with urine or, if growing wild in hedgerows, that it could have been sprayed with weed-killer or car exhaust fumes, then it should not be used. It is not safe in this state, however much it is washed before use. (See also *GREENFOOD.*)

H

ingredients can be obtained in a health food store.

>3 tablespoons high protein baby cereal
>1 tablespoon wheatgerm
>1 tablespoon millet meal
>1 tablespoon sunflower meal

HAND REARING

Sometimes, if both parents have died and there are no other pairs breeding with which you can foster the chick or chicks; or if for some reason the parents reject one particular youngster, it becomes necessary to try to rear the chick by hand. This is a task which requires a great deal of patience and dedication, but it can be done. A hand-reared chick, rather than a discarded dead youngster, from a breeding pair from whom the breeder expected his best results, is a great source of satisfaction. The older the baby is when hand-rearing commences, the more chance there is of success.

The baby bird is normally kept warm by the hen, at first tucked right underneath her where the temperature is around 32° C (90° F), and later close to her in a temperature of about 30° C (86° F). Some sort of substitute has to be found for this environment and it is unlikely that the average fancier has anything purpose-made available. A plastic cake tin with the lid left slightly open, and lined with crumpled tissues, is a possibility. This must be kept somewhere where the temperature can be controlled at that at which the chick appears comfortable. If it is too hot it will move about, lifting its wings, trying to get cool. If it is too cold, it will soon die. A thermometer, which can be checked constantly, is a necessity. If a hospital cage is available, the chick can be housed in a perspex basin which has first been warmed and then lined with tissues, and a tissue can be put on top of the chick. A bowl of water should be placed near the basin to prevent the air becoming too dry.

The following dry mixture should be reduced to a fine powder in a blender, then mixed with hot water to a thin cream and a tiny drop of a multi-vitamin added. The

This is given with a pipette and can be squirted directly down the gullet, which saves a lot of time, although it can be dangerous if any of the food should get into the windpipe. It is far better to let the baby suck it from the pipette itself, held to the beak, but a lot of patience is needed. It helps if the chick is held with a tissue wrapped around it to prevent any of the feed spilling onto the feathers, as it is sticky and sets fairly hard. The number of feeds needed per day depends upon the age of the chick. When very tiny, it needs to be fed almost every two hours during the day, and several times during the night, but when it is about three weeks old, once every four hours, with a late night and early morning feed, is plenty. After a few days, most youngsters can be persuaded to take the food from a spoon with the sides bent up to form a kind of scoop, which speeds up the feeding time required considerably.

Any food not used at one feed should be kept in the refrigerator and reheated when required. A suitable receptacle is the indentation in an egg poacher, and this cup, or eggcup, in which it is stored can be placed in a saucepan of boiling water until it reaches the right temperature. The food should be fairly warm but not so hot that it will burn the throat of the baby. The best method of testing is a few drops on one's own tongue. It is quite palatable.

HEAD QUALITY

The shape of the head plays an important part in deciding whether a bird will make a good show specimen. The spots may be large, the mask deep, the colour superlative, but unless the head is wide when viewed face on, has a frontal rise which continues in a graceful sweep over the top of the head and does not fall away at the

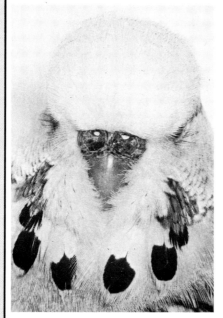

A bird with all the desirable head qualities.

back, it is unlikely to win against reasonable competition.

HEATING
From many observations and experiments, it appears that artificial heating is not absolutely essential as budgerigars seem to be able to breed successfully in very low temperatures. Some form of heating is desirable, however, for two reasons. Occasionally, temperatures plummet to well below zero and this can hardly be comfortable for very young babies, while if the temperature is kept at around 10° C (50° F), the birdroom is certainly far more comfortable for the fancier. Birds in inside flights with access to outside flights do not require any heating, but care must be taken to check that the water supply has not frozen.

Oil stoves and gas heaters should never be used for heating aviaries or birdhouses. Horror stories of birdrooms where the wicks of oil heaters have blown out, filling the room with filthy smoke which has slowly and painfully choked the lungs of the poor birds, until they have been found dead or dying in the morning, used to be heard in the past. Fortunately, almost every fancier has learned that the only safe methods of heating a birdroom are electric tubular heaters, electric oil-filled radiators, or some form of central heating radiators as an

extension from the central heating of the house. Whichever of these are used, it should be controlled by a thermostat. Unless the birdroom has been efficiently insulated, heating can be an expensive item.

HOSPITAL CAGE
A commercially bought hospital cage is a small, all-metal cage with a built-in heater and thermostat. Being of metal, it is easy to clean fastidiously and to disinfect. Its one disadvantage is that it is an alien environment for the sick bird and therefore likely to cause *stress*. A bird which is very ill has little interest in its surroundings, but if the bird is just 'off colour', it may be more beneficial to use a show cage with which it is familiar and to put this in a warm place. An ordinary thermometer can be used to try to ensure that the temperature is kept at around 29°C (85°F). Because heat tends to make a budgie thirsty, as does fever, a supply of water must always be available and if this is treated with any medicine, it is necessary to allow for the fact that the bird will drink more than usual and adjust the dose accordingly. A shallow container of water should be kept near the cage to counteract the air-drying effect of the heat of the hospital cage, or nearby fire or radiator. One word of warning: before leaving a cage in front of direct heat, first check the intensity

A hospital cage should be warm, but must never be too hot.

of the heat by holding the back of your hand in front of the cage, between the cage and the heat source, for about five minutes. If it is uncomfortable for your hand, it will be uncomfortable for the bird, and the cage should be moved back.

HUMIDITY

A degree of humidity is needed to keep the eggs from drying so much that the membranes just inside the shell toughen, making it impossible for the chick to break out of the shell, resulting in a lot of chicks *dead in shell*. In an average season in the UK, the temperature range is such, and the rainfall high enough, to make any additional form of humidity not an absolute necessity. However, in particularly dry seasons, or if the breeder decides to pair up his birds in the summer for some reason, and in many other countries, it is necessary to install a *humidifier* and *humidistat* to control the humidity of the air.

The vital humidity is that underneath the hen, but many believe that this is affected by the general humidity of the surrounding atmosphere.

HUSBANDRY

From the very first day of keeping birds, a routine should be established. The birds become used to it, it means that essential tasks are never overlooked and very often disasters can be avoided. If your hours of work permit, it is wise to visit the birdroom or aviary twice each day, once in the morning and again in early evening. First check over the outside of the flights, looking for any structural damage caused by cats, dogs or other visitors. Check that the wire netting is intact and there is nowhere that a bird could escape. Next, look along the perches at the birds to ensure that none are sitting hunched up, usually with head tucked around and both feet down. If there are, make a note of which ones they are and remember to take action as soon as you are inside the birdhouse. Next, look around the floor to make certain there are no sick or even dead birds lying anywhere.

Now go into the birdroom and carry out the same checks in the inside flights. If you discover any birds which look sick, catch them up and put each in a clean show cage or hospital cage. Cover the floor of this cage with dry seed and twist a millet spray around the bars. Fill a drinking fountain with water and fix this so that it can be reached even if the bird does not sit on the perch. Place the cage on the top of the central heating boiler or any other place where it will remain quite warm, but not uncomfortably so – and then wash your hands thoroughly. (Hands should always be washed, preferably with disinfectant in the water, after handling a sick or dead bird.)

The bird should be observed carefully over the next few hours. If it appears to be recovering, as they often do when kept in a warm place, leave it for two days and then move it further and further from the heat, until it is once again used to the sort of temperature at which you keep your birdroom, before releasing it back into the birdroom. If it shows no sign of recovery and symptoms appear which indicate a serious illness, the advice of a veterinary surgeon should be sought.

Once the health of the birds has been checked and any invalids have been ministered to, the seed dishes should be checked and topped up where necessary, then any soaked seeds or additives distributed. It is sensible to have feeding dishes which are large enough to avoid having to replenish them daily, both because the task is time-consuming and also in case of some emergency which might prevent you from visiting the birdroom on a particular day. Always start and finish your rounds at the same spot.

Once each week the flights should be cleaned of dust and all droppings removed. During the breeding season, the copious droppings of the hens should also be removed from the breeding cages.

Once every three months, one flight at a time should be emptied of birds and cleaned thoroughly with water to which a chlorous type of disinfectant has been added. Walls, perches and floor should be washed.

To prevent mite and any build up of moths or other insects, twice a year, preferably in late spring and early autumn, the inside flights, after removal of the birds, should be sprayed with one of the special sprays sold for this purpose, or with water containing Duramitex. The smell of this is dreadful, but it does prevent any sign of mite. No birds should be returned to the flight until it is completely dry.

Once breeding has been completed and the birds transferred to the flights, the breeding cages should be brushed out, scrubbed, disinfected and painted with paint which has been mixed with one of the anti-mite products.

I

IDEAL BUDGERIGAR

Most budgerigar societies throughout the world describe or illustrate a standard of excellence for what they consider to be the ideal budgerigar. The differences in the written descriptions are usually minor, while the pictorial representation can differ according to the interpretation of the artist. The written standard for the United Kingdom is set by the Budgerigar Society and reads as follows:

CONDITION is essential. If a bird is not in condition it should *never* be considered for any award.

TYPE – Gracefully tapered from nape of neck to tip of tail, with an approximately straight back line and a rather deep, nicely curved chest.

LENGTH – The ideal length is eight-and-a-half inches [22 cm] from the crown of the head to the tip of the tail.

WINGS – Carried just above the cushion of the tail and not crossed. The ideal length of the wing is three-and-three-quarter inches [9.5 cm] from the butt to the tip of the longest primary flight which must contain seven visual primary flight feathers fully grown.

HEAD – Large, round wide and symmetrical when viewed from any angle; curvature of skull commencing at cere, to lift outward and upward, continuing over the top and to the base of head in one graceful sweep.

BEAK – Set well into the face.

EYE – To be bold and bright and positioned well away from the front, top and back skull.

NECK – To be short and wide when viewed from either side or front.

TAIL – To be straight and tight with two long tail feathers.

POSITION – Steady, on perch, at an angle of 30 degrees from the vertical, looking fearless and natural.

MASK AND SPOTS – Mask to be clear, deep and wide, and where

These wooden models by R. Harris depict his interpretation of the ideal shape of a cock and hen. The male has a noticeably deeper chest.

demanded by the Standard should be ornamented by six evenly spaced large round throat spots, the outer two being partially covered at the base by cheek patches, the size of spots to be in proportion to the rest of the make-up of the bird.

LEGS AND FEET – Legs should be straight and strong, with two front and two rear toes and claws firmly gripping perch.

MARKINGS – Wavy markings on cheek, head, neck, back and wings to stand out clearly.

COLOUR – Clear and level and of an even shade.

IN-BREEDING

In-breeding should never be attempted by beginners, because while it may stabilise desirable features carried by the parents, it can also double-up on any faults which they may be carrying and some of those faults may be hidden. The mating of mother to son, father to daughter, brother to sister, or first cousin to first cousin are what is understood by in-breeding. Mating of more distantly related birds comes under the heading of *line-breeding*. A very careful check should be made by those practising in-breeding that the stock which they use is selected for fertility. If in-breeding is used on stock already showing poor fertility, this feature will be exaggerated as each generation is in-bred, until eventually no further progeny will be produced because the birds will have become sterile.

The aim of in-breeding is to increase, and then stabilise, particular desirable features in a fancier's stock. He may, for example, have a bird with very large, perfectly round and even spots which he wishes to stabilise into his stud – and this is possible. He should, however, be conversant with the history of the large-spotted bird and should not attempt to commence in-breeding with it unless detailed records have been kept. If some hereditary defect were to be carried by this bird and also by its partner, then, as well as large spots, the breeder might be introducing flecked heads, or poor markings or some other fault. Provided that the breeder is experienced and has kept meticulous records, he may achieve surprising improvement in show quality by in-breeding. This has been demonstrated particularly in South Africa where there are few breeders and they were unable to import outcrosses to improve their stock.

The beginner to in-breeding should choose very carefully the birds with which he intends to establish a family. Having chosen a pair, he should look back through his records to find out if any faults have been recorded – in appearance, in breeding habits – or any weaknesses which have appeared regularly for several years. Any bird without an excellent pedigree should be discarded. If an *outcross* is being sought, it should be explained to the seller that the purpose is to start in-breeding and he should be asked if he will search his records to make sure that the bird being bought has a good pedigree. After the first breeding season, the youngsters should be examined carefully. Any displaying any of the major faults should be discarded from the future breeding team.

Once the birds have moulted out and are in their full adult plumage, the wisest plan is to cage each family, parents and offspring, to judge what progress, if any, has been made. If the youngsters are an improvement on their parents and are carrying no major faults, then it is safe to continue with that family as part of your in-breeding team. If, on the other hand, the progeny are of poorer quality than their parents, or have crossed wings, drooping tails, heavy flecking, or any bad show point, they should be ruthlessly discarded. Only patience and dedication lead to the top and it is no use hoping that birds which have produced bad specimens one year will suddenly cure themselves of all their faults the following season.

INCUBATION
The normal period of incubation for a budgerigar egg is eighteen days. Eggs are laid on alternate days and, subsequently, also hatch every other day. Usually the hen starts to incubate the egg as soon as it has been laid, but there are always exceptions to the rule and some hens will lay two or three eggs before starting to incubate, which can interfere with the sequence of hatching.

There is very little likelihood of difficulty during the incubation period. Provided that the hen is fit, she will sit quite contentedly in the nest box, coming out only to feed or defecate. The cock, as a general rule, sits outside in the breeding cage, feeds the hen and, when she emerges from the nest box is attentive and affectionate. Sometimes a cock will stay in the box with the hen, quite quietly and seemingly quite welcome. On very rare occasions, a cock will become troublesome, disturbing the hen so constantly that she is unable to incubate the eggs and becomes quarrelsome. If this is observed, it is better to remove the cock for most of each day and, if the trouble continues even after the chicks begin to hatch, when he should be kept busy feeding the hen, he can be removed altogether and the hen allowed to bring up the chicks on her own. In this case, it is wise to foster some of the chicks when they are old enough to ring, leaving the hen with only two chicks to rear.

Hens can, and have, hatched clutches of up to nine eggs, although four or five are more usual. As the temperature just around the hen is considerably lower than the temperature just underneath her, where she actually incubates, it is not surprising that eggs which are on the perimeter of her so-called 'incubation pad' fail to hatch.

INFERTILITY
The causes of infertility are many, and very often a pair who have not produced are wrongly labelled infertile. As more research is carried out into the production of eggs, the reasons for eggs being *addled* or *dead in shell*, and even, recently, into *artificial insemination*, many new facts have emerged. It has been found that the cocks have a cycle during part of which they produce either no sperm or immature sperm and when the testes are tiny, in comparison to what is needed to produce the semen, alive with sperm, which is needed to ensure the fertilisation of the egg. If the cock is put down to breed during the 'resting' period, he is unlikely to fertilise the hen's eggs and may,

mistakenly, be thought to be infertile. Two things help to bring him back into breeding condition; they are extra light and the call of the hen. Extra artificial lighting can help with both, since the hen will call more often during the hours of light.

One of the other reasons for apparent infertility is that the perches in the breeding cage may be too smooth. If round dowelling is

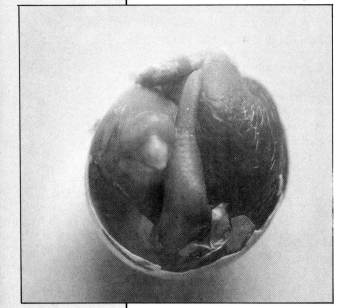

An unborn chick that is dead in its shell.

used for perches, sometimes the hen is unable to grip the perch and the cock literally falls off before copulation can occur. The answer to this problem is to fit square perches.

Coarse feathering around the hen's vent area can sometimes prevent efficient copulation, no matter how fertile the pair. One possible answer to this is to pluck the feathers away from the vent area – very, very carefully – or to trim them with scissors.

There are other reasons for *clear*, or apparently clear, eggs. Some infection may be present in the nest box which kills off the embryo before it can start to develop; the hen may not be incubating properly because she is being disturbed by the cock, by mice in the birdroom, or by flashing lights or unusual night noises. All possible causes should be examined before a bird is dubbed infertile.

INO FACTOR
The ino factor has the effect of masking all the genes of the green series birds, to produce the lutino, and all the genes of the blue series birds, except one, to produce the albino. The one gene in the blue series which the ino factor seems incapable of masking is the yellow face. When these two genes are present in one bird, a yellow face albino is the result. Although the ino gene appears to be dominant to all colours, it does not affect varieties. Tufted or crested lutinos and albinos are quite commonplace.

INSULATION
Adequate insulation is advisable, both for the comfort of the birds and the fancier who will spend much time in his birdroom, and also from the point of view of economy. The heat loss from a birdroom or aviary which is not insulated is very considerable. A thick layer of insulation between the outer and inner walls and in the roof space is a good long-term investment. Care must be taken not to use an insulating material which could become a warren of nests for rodents. This is prevented by using a material which would be very uncomfortable, such as rockwool or fibre glass.

INTERMEDIATE
An intermediate is an exhibitor who has passed through the beginner and novice sections and is now allowed a further four years, or six wins, in full classes at open shows before moving into the final, champion section. For many years this section has been weak in numbers – though quite strong in quality – because many people who have originally taken up the hobby, have given up for various reasons along the way. Most fanciers who pass successfully through the intermediate section to become champions, remain fanciers for life.

J

judges the same classes and records his results. The two papers are sent to an evaluating panel who notify the success or failure to the applicant.

JUDGES' PANELS

The rules for inclusion in judges' panels vary throughout the world. These rules are set by the controlling organisation; in the UK the Budgerigar Society, in the USA the American Budgerigar Society, and similarly in all countries where shows are organised. The Budgerigar Society has two levels of judges; the subsidiary panel whose members are allowed individually to judge shows at a lower patronage level, and the main panel. To achieve subsidiary panel status, a person must have been a member of the Budgerigar Society for not less than ten years and must be currently exhibiting as a champion. To reach the standard needed for the main panel, he must have judged at least nine classes over three years under the supervision of main panel judges, and then pass both practical and written examinations. Once elevated to the main panel, the judge must continue to breed and exhibit birds annually and must remain a paid-up member of the Budgerigar Society.

Area societies in the UK have the right to form their own judges' panels for their own areas. The rules for acceptance for these, in most cases, are simply to have been a member of the society for a set number of years.

In the USA the applicant for a judges' panel must be a champion and must have obtained a number of wins at shows in separate years. He then needs a sponsoring club and recommendations from three established judges. He begins his apprenticeship by accompanying a judge throughout a show, and finishes by taking a practical test in which he is asked to judge three different classes or sections with five different groups of birds, while the judge is out of the room, recording his results which are kept confidential. The official judge then

JUDGING RULES

Each country differs slightly in its judging rules, but all endeavour to ensure absolute fairness for the exhibitors. Cages are recognised only by cage numbers or tags which give no indication of the owner of the bird and no judge is allowed to discover the owners until after all judging has been completed. In the UK judges are not allowed to stay overnight with an exhibitor before a show, and it would be unethical for him to visit an exhibitor's birdroom where he might see the exhibits. A bird cannot be exhibited if it was bought from the judge who will be adjudicating at the show, and no judge is allowed to show budgerigars at a show at which he is adjudicating, even if he is scheduled to judge a different colour or section from that in which he would be liable to exhibit. The only exception to this rule is that a subsidiary panel judge may exhibit at a show at which he is taking his training because none of his placings affect the final results.

JUNIORS

An exhibitor is allowed to show in junior classes from the age of ten to sixteen years. During the whole year in which he reaches his sixteenth birthday, he remains eligible for junior classes. As with the other sections, if he should show in a higher class, he cannot then revert to junior status. One condition placed upon this section is that no one may show in junior classes if anyone living at the same address is showing budgerigars in a higher section.

L

LACEWINGS

As the name implies, the markings on a lacewing are lighter than those of the normal varieties. They are red-eyed, sex-linked birds with a clear body colour of yellow or white and light cinnamon markings on head, neck, mask and wings. Although of attractive appearance, these birds have not become popular on the show bench because they tend to be much smaller than their normal counterparts.

LAYING, SIGNS OF

Once the birds have been paired up and a nest box provided, if all is well, the hen will begin to investigate the nest box. Her visits will become more frequent and the periods spent inside will become longer. Sometimes the fancier sees mating taking place, but not always, and this is not important. Remember, no one can be watching for 24 hours a day. Two of the tell-tale signs that the hen will soon lay are that she begins to tap on the nest-box walls and she attempts to chew the nest-box hole. At the lower part of the hen's body, behind the legs, it will become noticeable (usually on the sixth or seventh day after pairing) that the area is slightly enlarged and, at the same time, the droppings will change from the normal, small black and white pieces to much heavier, softer deposits, roughly six times larger than during the rest of the year. These heavy droppings will continue throughout the laying and incubation period, allowing the hen to remain in the nest box for long periods without the need to come out to defecate.

LEGS

The legs of a young budgerigar are usually a light, fleshy colour – with the normal varieties they darken as they become older, until, at about one year old, they are greyish with a much rougher surface. The legs of a young budgerigar are fragile and easily damaged. Whilst in the nest box they may become fouled by excreta which quickly hardens. This should not be picked off, because it is so easy to break or hurt a leg. It can, however, be soaked off quite easily using a piece of soft cloth and warm water.

Problems with the legs can sometimes arise as the birds get older. A piece of sawdust, grit, scale or other foreign body can get caught inside the closed ring. This can make a tiny abrasion which becomes infected, resulting in a swollen leg. If this goes undetected, the bird could be lost or, at the least, suffer a great deal of pain and discomfort. Observing the birds for any signs of illness or discomfort is always very important.

If a bird with a swollen leg is discovered, iodine ointment should be applied twice daily and a hot wet cloth held around the leg as a poultice for about five minutes. If, after two days, the swelling has not reduced, the ring should be cut off. A pair of very short nail clippers is a very useful tool for this task. Anyone without experience should not attempt to cut off a ring because it is possible to break the leg or cause excess bleeding. Help should be sought from an experienced breeder or from a veterinary surgeon. When cutting off a ring, the ring should be held absolutely steady in a pair of narrow pliers. If it should twist, it could break the leg or pierce the swollen flesh. It is always useful to have a second person to hold the bird for this operation. It is advisable to make two cuts and the two portions will then come away quite easily.

If a sitting hen should develop a swollen leg, the ring should be cut off immediately this is noticed since it is not feasible to keep her under supervision and observe the progress she is making.

Once rings are removed, it is no longer possible to win some awards, but the health and comfort of the birds must be the prime consideration.

LICE

Known as *feather lice*, these parasites burrow to the base of the feathers and can cause tremendous irritation. A bird infected with these lice will continually pick at its feathers, to such an extent that bare patches will appear. It is very difficult to trace the lice as they live beneath the feathers, close to the skin. If the condition is suspected, the bird should be washed daily in warm soapy water to which a mild disinfectant has been added, taking care not to allow this to get into the eyes. Eight or nine days are usually sufficient to clear the lice. The patient's partner should also be observed for signs of feather picking. If necessary, it too should be treated. The nest box should be sprayed with a strong *anti-mite solution* such as Duramitex before the birds are put in again. If the affected bird has come from the main flights, then all the others should be watched for signs of lice and the flight thoroughly cleaned, disinfected and sprayed with an anti-mite solution. (See *DISINFECTANTS*.)

LIGHTING

Lighting is almost a necessity, to enable the breeder to tend to the needs of his stock during the winter months before he goes to work and after he returns. It is also an aid to giving more hours of light to the birds, which helps to bring them into breeding condition. It is advisable to have a 1.5 m (5 ft) fluorescent fitting for every 2.5 m (8 ft) in length of the birdroom. A *night light* is not a luxury; it can help settle the birds down during a storm or any other disturbance, and allows the breeding hen sufficient light to find food during the night when she is feeding young chicks. The most useful types of night lights are those which connect to the mains, but have a built-in transformer which reduces the voltage to 12v or 6v. This also reduces the amount of heat, which is a safety factor. No one should attempt to put in this wiring unless he is a competent electrician, but should engage a qualified tradesman instead.

LINE BREEDING

Descriptions of line breeding often differ very little from *in-breeding*, but the generally accepted view is that line breeding means using birds not quite so closely related. Mother to son, father to daughter or sister to brother are accepted as in-breeding, while cousin to aunt or uncle, half sister to half brother, etc., are believed to be line breeding. The same rules apply to both. The breeder must be experienced before attempting this type of breeding and he must have available to him comprehensive records going back for several generations, giving information on any fault which may have been carried by the family. Once two or three lines, or families, have been established, the best progeny of each are mated together to produce a better quality of show stock than the original pairings. As the relationships used in line breeding are not close, the procedure can be carried on for a number of generations before the lines become too closely interrelated and new families need to be established.

LIST OF MEMBERS

For beginners coming into the budgerigar fancy, or for any member who is travelling, a list of other members is of immense interest. Most of the area societies publish lists of members in their area and the Budgerigar Society publishes a handbook which gives the names and addresses of all members. As many keen overseas fanciers are members of the UK Budgerigar Society, even those travelling overseas are able to contact fellow fanciers on their journeys, and often do so. The American Budgerigar Society, and a number of other overseas budgerigar clubs, have lists of members available for visitors to their countries.

LOSS OF FEATHERS

There are a number of causes of feather loss. In very young chicks, the cause is usually *French moult*, which is described elsewhere in the book. *Feather lice* could be the culprits, with the bird pecking out its feathers due to the intense irritation. Yet another cause could be one of the *skin diseases* caused by moulds, such as *ringworm*, described under disease. Should any of these lesions be present, treatment with an anti-fungal cream should be continued until all signs have disappeared. Except in the case of French moult, if a bird begins to lose feathers, or develop bald patches, it should be caught up and examined carefully for any skin trouble. If none is apparent, then lice should be suspected and the recommended treatment carried out.

LUTINOS

A lutino is a bird of the green series with the addition of an ino gene. This masks the underlying colour, leaving a bird of an all over vivid yellow colour. The object of all lutino breeders, having achieved a high standard of show-style budgerigars, is to improve the colour until it reaches an almost orangey shade known as 'hot yellow'. The lutino is one of the sex-linked variety of birds. It has red eyes with white iris rings and the legs and feet are a fleshy pink.

M

MARKINGS

In some varieties certain markings must be present to comply with the standard for the variety; in other varieties, certain of the markings must be absent or almost invisible. To become a successful exhibitor of a variety, it is important that the breeder learns about those markings which apply to that variety. To become a judge, all the stipulations for colour and markings must be assimilated. All the standards are given in the handbook of the Budgerigar Society in the UK, or in the publications of the relevant ruling bodies in other countries.

MASK

Ideally, the face of a show budgerigar should be the size of a circle 2.5 cm (1 in) in diameter. The lower part of the face, below the beak, is known as the mask. In the green series birds it is yellow, and in the blue series (except the yellow face blues) it is white.

The depth of colour undoubtedly enhances the mask, which can, on occasions, be too pale. It should be wide and deep, with six evenly spaced round spots at the lower edge.

A multi-spotted opaline budgerigar with an untrimmed mask.

78

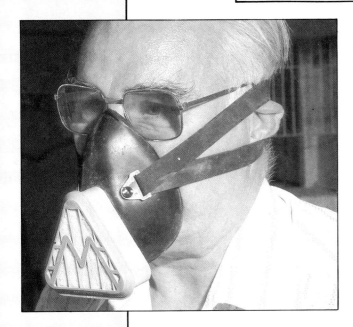

A protective mask is recommended to anyone with asthma or other breathing or chest ailments.

other areas with water before cleaning, helps to combat the dust problem.

MATING
Sometimes mating can even be observed in the nursery flight, when the youngsters are only ten weeks old, while when breeding-fit birds are first put into the breeding cages, it is not uncommon for a pair to mate within minutes. Conversely, some pairs, while successful in breeding, are never seen to mate.

Mating normally takes place on the perch. The hen lies across the perch, making her back concave and lifting her tail so that the feathering around the vent is opened, avoiding any obstruction. The cock mounts onto the back of the hen, arching his back and positioning his tail below hers. After a successful act of copulation, the cock returns to his perch, while the hen remains motionless for a few seconds. Mating usually takes place in the early morning, as soon as the lights are turned on, and it is not uncommon for a pair to mate several times.

MASKS, PROTECTIVE
Dust from budgerigars kept in large numbers can be irritating to some breeders' lungs. Dust particles of a reasonable size are usually trapped by the cilia in the nose or upper respiratory tract and are coughed or blown away, but small particles can be inhaled and the tiniest particles can reach the alveoli of the lungs where they can cause trouble. Anyone who suffers from asthma or other breathing problems or chest diseases, is advised to wear a mask when cleaning out cages and flights where a lot of dust is created. The mask covers the nose and mouth, but allows easy breathing. Spraying the floors of flights, nest boxes or

MEDICINES
There are many simple types of medicines which can be given to cage birds for a number of complaints, but the inexperienced should never 'try' *antibiotics* for which they know neither the dosage or the specific use. If warmth and simple medicines do not effect a speedy improvement in a sick bird, the professional advice of a veterinary surgeon should be sought.

If a bird cuts itself on a sharp piece of metal or wire, the small wound can become infected and an abscess will result. *Tincture of iodine*, painted on twice a day, will often cause these little abscesses to disappear. Should they remain, bathing the affected part for five or ten minutes with fairly hot water to which has been added a little iodine, may cause the abscess to burst. If this doesn't happen and the swelling has come to a head, it should be pricked with a sterile needle and carefully washed with salt and warm water until it is clean. A little

A budgerigar cock which has had its mask trimmed ready for a show. This task should be done a few days before exhibiting the bird to allow the feathers to settle.

penicillin ointment, applied twice daily, will ensure clean healing.

A bird with a cold or cough shows similar symptoms to a human. The nostrils exude mucous, the eyes sometimes water, the breathing is wheezy and the bird looks fluffed up and generally sorry for itself. It should be kept isolated in a warm place and seven or eight drops of a pleasant tasting cough medicine, such as that sold for human babies, can be added to its drinking water.

A useful medicine to keep in the aviary medicine chest is cold, black, unsugared tea for simple diarrhoea. Alf Ormerod, one of the world's most experienced breeders, states that it should be made by first using a tea bag in the normal way – and then drinking the tea yourself. Then use the tea bag for the second time, to make a strong infusion to be used in place of water for the sick bird. Unless this is kept in a refrigerator, the mixture should be thrown away and a new supply made quite frequently.

Other medicines which should be kept in the birds' medicine box are sulphur ointment for the treatment of scaly face or scaly leg. Ordinary eye lotion or tablets, as sold for humans, can be kept for use as eye drops for eyes which are red and which are obviously causing the bird discomfort. The cause of this is often a tiny piece of seed husk or sand which has slipped under the lid, or else the bird may have been in a draught. A miniature bottle of brandy is useful for birds which have a chill or have been badly frightened. Six drops are added to three tablespoons of water and used in the drinker.

Two antibiotic creams which are very useful, but have to be obtained under prescription from a doctor or vet, are Terramycin Ophthalmic which is very effective against any pus-forming organisms and useful for sinusitis; and penicillin ointment for use on any infected wounds.

Budgerigars often suffer from iodine deficiency and a course of extra iodine is useful. Care must be taken not to overdose; two drops in 0.5 litre (1 pt) of water is all that is needed. The treatment should be continued for three weeks for maximum benefit.

A small bottle of a multi-vitamin preparation is useful as a tonic and is valuable for use after a bird has been treated with an antibiotic.

Liquid paraffin, for use if egg-binding occurs or as a mild laxative is useful.

Sucrose added to the water also acts as a mild purgative if a bird is constipated.

MENDELIAN THEORY

Around 1860, long before genes had been discovered, Gregor Mendel, an Austrian monk, conducted a series of tests using garden peas. He crossed dwarf peas with tall peas and produced all tall peas; he self-pollinated these and produced 75 per cent tall and 25 per cent dwarf. Self-pollinating again, he found all the dwarf variety bred true: 30 per cent of the tall variety bred true and the remainder of the tall variety gave 75 per cent tall and 25 per cent dwarf again. He continued with these experiments and added further complications. He saw that some of the plants had green seed, while others had wrinkled and yellow seeds. He produced tables showing that some varieties were dominant and others recessive. He proved that although two varieties could be of the visual dominant variety, if they were both carrying the recessive feature in a hidden or split form, the two recessives could join together and produce a plant or a seed of the recessive variety. In all, Mendel studied seven pairs of characters in peas, all of which proved that his original theories were correct. Sixty-five years later, two scientists who were also greatly interested in budgerigars, Dr H. Duncker and Consul General Cremer of Germany, applied Mendel's theories to colour in budgerigars and produced tables giving the expectations from every possible mating of budgerigars known at that time. These tables are still in use today, listed in the Budgerigar Society book Budgerigar Matings and Colour Expectations. Every serious breeder needs a copy of this book for reference.

A humane mouse-catching device. Once the mice have entered, they cannot escape and can later be released, unharmed, into the wild.

MIRRORS

If, for any reason, a pet bird has to be left in a cage without company for any length of time, there is no doubt that it becomes lonely and the best substitute for its owner/companion is a mirror. It will talk to its mirror, play with its mirror and feed its mirror (for this reason the mirror must be frequently washed). Mirrors of all sizes, with bells or other toys attached, can be bought from pet shops. The wisest choice is a mirror made from polished steel, because if this is pulled out and dropped in play, it will not break leaving minute slivers of glass which could be picked up by the budgie .

MITE

The most common variety of mite which can infest breeding establishments is the *red mite* or *roost mite*. During the day it is grey in colour and hides in cracks and crevices or under nest-box blocks. At night, the blood-sucking creatures emerge to gorge on the blood of the birds. The poor hen sitting in the nest box, and the young chicks, are favourite targets. These blood-sucking forays of the agile mite can cause serious *anaemia* and loss of weight. When there is bad infestation, an early morning visit, when lights first go on, may show patches of blood-filled bright red mites which have not had time to scuttle away to their daytime hideaways. The mite can be brought into the aviary by new stock, or come from wild birds perching on the wires and shedding a few of their mites which very quickly multiply.

No one interested in his birds will want them to become infested with these blood-sucking parasites, and prevention is better than cure. They will not live long if all the breeding cages have been thoroughly sprayed with an *acaricide*, such as Duramitex, or a preparation containing hexachloride, malathion, pyrethrum or derris root, or a combination of these, and then painted with paint impregnated with the same.

If red mites are found, the birds should be caught up, very quickly sprayed with one of the proprietary

MICE

Mice and budgerigars do not co-exist in harmony. The droppings and urine of the rodents are poisonous to the birds, and mice have even been known to nibble off the feet of tiny babies. Every sensible precaution should be taken to ensure that mice never get into a birdroom or flight and that no seed or foodstuff is contaminated by their excreta. If any sign of mice is found, their source of ingress should be discovered and blocked as quickly as possible and every mouse inside the birdhouse caught and destroyed. Traps for this purpose are widely advertised in the fancy press.

MINERALS

Most of the mineral requirements of a budgerigar are contained in its normal diet. Manganese, magnesium, phosphorus, sulphur and potassium are all found in budgerigar seeds; iron is found in greenfoods, in wholemeal bread, oats and eggs; sodium and chloride are obtainable from oats, bread and cuttlefish. The only mineral necessary for health, which does not occur naturally in the budgerigar's diet, appears to be iodine and that can be supplied by iodine nibblets or through seed soaked in a very mild solution of Vanodine.

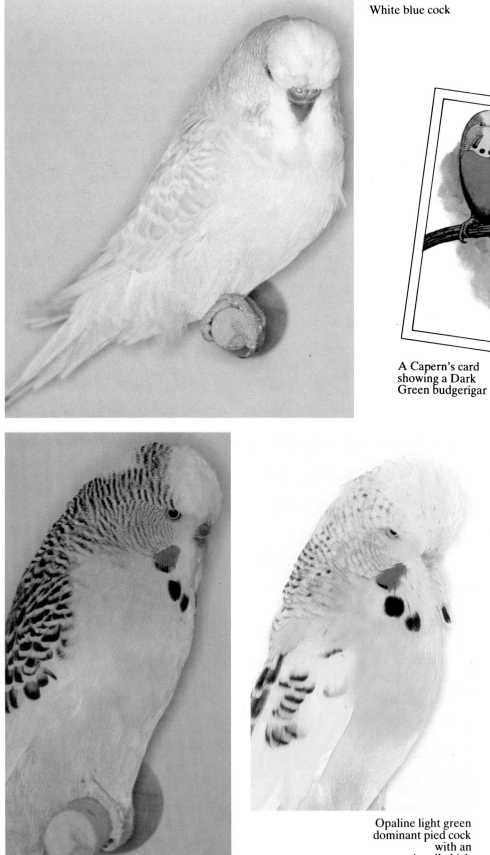

White blue cock

A Capern's card
showing a Dark
Green budgerigar

Light green
dominant pied cock
showing a clear
yellow band just
above the thighs

Opaline light green
dominant pied cock
with an
exceptionally high
frontal rise

Eye-catching varieties

Dark green
dominant pied cock

mite-killing sprays which are harmless to birds or chicks (pyrethrum-based sprays are the safest kind), and transferred to a clean cage which has first been sprayed with an anti-mite preparation and given a new nest box. The old nest box should be emptied and the sawdust or other litter burned. The nest box can then be thoroughly soaked, disinfected and treated with an anti-mite preparation before reuse. The husks and litter from the breeding cage should also be burned and the perches and inside of the cage scrubbed with a strong solution of disinfectant and then treated with a spray containing an anti-mite preparation. Careful watch must be kept on all adjacent cages, because red mite are agile, long-legged

A red mite showing the long legs which give these parasites their agility.

creatures which very quickly migrate to pastures new. They can live for a long time – a matter of months – away from their unwitting hosts and without a feed of blood. Constant watchfulness is necessary until the end of the breeding season, when the breeding room can be emptied and thoroughly mite-proofed before the next season.

MOULTING

A soft moult can occur at any time of the year. It can be brought on by a change in the weather; it can occur when the birds are first put back into the flights after the breeding season; it can happen immediately after a show, when the birds have been taken to a hall where the temperature is totally different from that of their normal environment. In a soft moult, the bird loses a number of feathers, but very seldom the main flights or tail feathers.

At about four months of age, a baby budgerigar goes through its first moult. In the normal varieties, it loses all the 'baby' feathers from above the beak to the top of its head.

The new feathers which grow are of a clear colour with none of the baby *striations* or bars, and at the same time the white iris rings appear around the pupils of its eyes. When the new feathers regrow, they are usually a deeper colour than the nest feathers.

In a pet bird, where the temperature of its environment is kept almost even throughout the year, the moult can occur at any time, but often takes place in late spring or early summer when central heating is first turned off, creating a different, sometimes cooler, temperature for a short time.

In the UK the main, or annual moult, usually takes place in the autumn. The commencement can differ by as much as six weeks from the north of the country to the south, but as soon as the temperatures begin to drop the birds begin to lose feathers. They take between six and eight weeks to complete this moult. The first sign of the moult is that the birds lose body weight, then feathers, and at this time they are more susceptible to catching colds and chills. At the very first sign of the beginning of the annual moult, the birds should be fed with seed which has been treated with cod liver oil emulsion (see *FEEDING*). During this stage, the birds need good wholesome seed, some millet sprays as a titbit, and plenty of rest and quiet. *Calcium* should always be available in the form of cuttlefish and oystershell grit.

Additional hours of artificial light seem to hasten the process of the moult, but it is not advised because then it seems not to be quite complete. If the birds are 'forced' through the moult, their bodies seem not to be fully and naturally prepared for the rigours of early breeding, whereas if they are allowed only natural daylight during September and October, they seem to lose more feathers and then come through into tiptop breeding condition. As they begin to grow new feathers, their activity increases. Although they are not fully feather-fit for showing, their extra activity shows that the moult is almost over and they are beginning to come into breeding condition.

Sometimes a bird will moult very severely and lose a number of flight feathers at the same time, causing it to experience difficulty in flying. Any birds in this condition should be caught and caged in stock cages until they are fully able to fly again.

If it is desired to delay the moult of show birds in very good condition, they should be regularly sprayed with tepid water. This is, however, a temporary measure and nature will again take its course after a short period.

MUTATIONS

Although it seems incredible when one attends a bird show and sees the miscellany of colours and varieties of budgerigars on display, all of them are descended from the original wild green Australian birds which were first introduced into the UK in the early 1840s. Some of the mutations occurred in the wild, but many of them have occurred throughout the years in private birdrooms and aviaries.

Surprisingly, when these new mutations appear in one stud, they often happen simultaneously in another, sometimes in a different country. When a new mutation first appears, the birds are zealously sought after and the prices charged can be phenomenal. Skyblues, which were first seen in 1910, were sold at prices in excess of £100 each – a large amount of money at that time. Greywings, clearwings, lutinos and pieds all commanded high prices when they first appeared. The newest mutation to become popular in the UK is the spangle, but news is being received from Australia of brownwings and other new varieties. Two mutations which have not appeared naturally, but which many breeders have attempted to produce, are an all-black or black-winged bird, and the red budgerigar. Someone somewhere is hoping to make a fortune some day by breeding these varieties.

NEST BOXES

For many years after budgerigars were introduced into the UK, nest boxes were made from empty coconut shells with a hole cut for the birds to go in and out. Whilst the birds obviously found these satisfactory, the same could hardly be said for the breeder who had no idea of how many eggs were laid or whether they were fertile, until he saw the youngsters leave the nest.

Nest boxes now can be found in a variety of shapes and sizes and are normally made of plywood or softwood. The latter is recommended, particularly that used for floorboards: it helps to absorb moisture when the chicks are growing and it has good insulating properties which helps to keep the nest box warm. The hen can chew at the box with no fear that she might eat glue which can happen when plywood is used. An ideal size is 30 x 21.5 x 16.5 cm (12 x 8½ x 7¼ in) externally.

Carpentry skills do not need to be of a high standard to construct these nest boxes. It is, in effect, a room for the hen, a room in which she must feel secure, for she will spend many hours at a stretch sitting or sleeping in the nest box. To make a simple box with a let-down front, cut two pieces of board, 30 x 21.5 cm (12 x 8½ in) for the back and front, two pieces 30 x 14.5 cm (12 x 5⅝ in) for the top and bottom, and two side pieces of 17 x 14.5 cm (6⅞ x 5⅝ in). If the box is to be hung onto the front of the cage, an entrance hole, on a level with the space cut from the wire front, should be cut in the back panel. The hole should not be so large as to make the hen feel insecure, nor so small that she might damage herself while going in and out of the box. About 4 cm (1¾ in) is the right size for the normal show bird.

Back, top, bottom and sides are now nailed together. The front panel

The cinnamon factor

Cinnamon grey
green cock

Player's Cigarettes

Yellow Budgerigar

Opaline cinnamon
skyblue hen

A Fallow Light
Green budgerigar
on a Capern's card

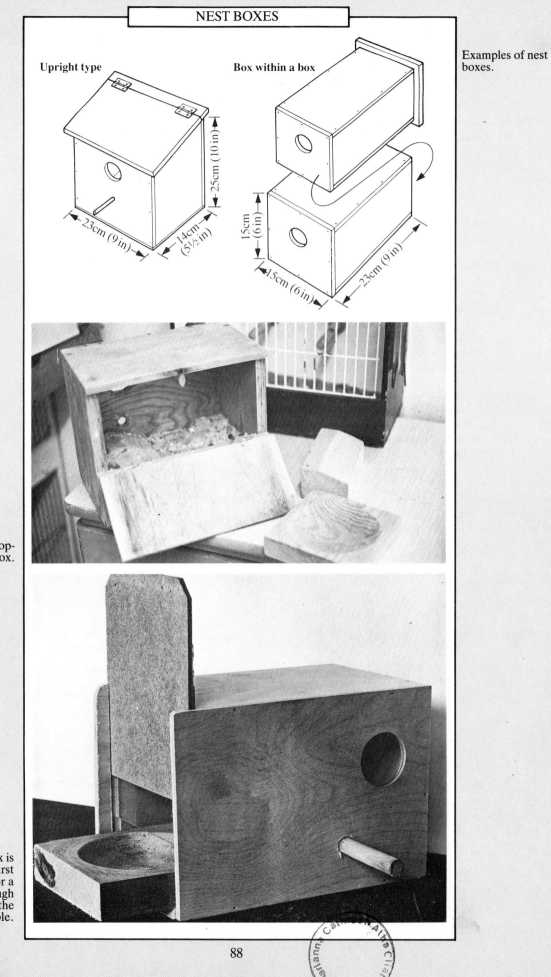

Upright type

Box within a box

25cm (10 in)

23cm (9 in) 14cm (5½ in)

15cm (6 in)

15cm (6 in) 23cm (9 in)

Examples of nest boxes.

The popular drop-front nest box.

This type of box is often the first choice for a beginner although it may not be the most suitable.

Compartment box with lift-up lid.

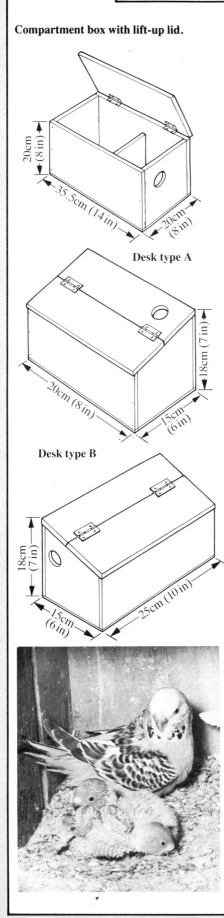

Desk type A

Desk type B

20cm (8 in)
35.5cm (14 in)
20cm (8 in)

18cm (7 in)
20cm (8 in)
15cm (6 in)

18cm (7 in)
15cm (6 in)
25cm (10 in)

is cut in two pieces, approximately 13 cm (5 in) from the top and hinges fixed to the outside to enable it to be dropped for the inspection of the nest box. It is then fastened at the top with luggage clasps. Two or three 10 mm (⅜ in) holes should be drilled high up on each end to provide ventilation. It cannot be stressed too firmly that when the box is hung up for use, it must be absolutely secure. It is normally held by two rings which fit onto two screws on the breeding cage front.

The position of the nest box does not seem to matter to most hens in high breeding condition, although there are some who will not enter the box unless it is in their preferred position. Boxes can be seen on the floors of cages, hung inside cages and even propped up on a perch inside some cages. Provided that the hen feels comfortable and secure, she will usually breed successfully. Wherever the nest box is positioned, it is beneficial to have the entrance hole facing away from the light, creating a box which is dark, though not completely black, inside.

Other types of nest boxes in general use are the desk type, top entry, deep open front and box-within-a-box.

Nest boxes are usually varnished or painted on the outside with emulsion paint, but should be left unpainted inside as the hen, and possibly the babies, will often eat the wood.

NEST BOX MATERIAL

For many years budgerigars were bred in nest boxes which contained nothing but a hardwood concave. This was a block of wood which covered the bottom of the nest box. The end away from the entrance hole had a depression, or concave, cut into it where the hen would lay and hatch her eggs. It was felt that this most resembled the breeding habits of wild budgerigars who build their nests in holes in hollow trees, and it was perfectly satisfactory and successful. Further research revealed that the trees used were usually rotten so that the hen could gnaw away a form of sawdust if she wished to line her nest.

Yellow suffused hen.

Rarer varieties

Spangle light green cock.

Two Capern's cards showing a light green budgerigar and a greywing cobalt budgerigar.

Player's Cigarettes

Mauve Greywing Budgerigar

Opaline greywing hen.

Now all manner of nest material is used by fanciers hoping to achieve the correct level of humidity to ensure the optimum hatching of eggs. Grass turf, peat and garden soil have all been used, apparently with success. Cloth material and fire ashes have been less successful. The most popular nesting materials are now sawdust or wood shavings. Those using wood shavings tend to fill the box and let the hen throw out what she does not want or need, so that she has sufficient material to make her nest as deep or shallow as she wishes.

A recommended filling for the nest box is first a sprinkling of *carbolic powder* to ensure that should the hen be carrying any type of mite, this will not have the opportunity to breed and multiply. Then a piece of wood 13 x 7.5 x 5 cm (5 x 3 x 2 in) is placed beneath the entrance hole for the hen to land on when she enters, and next two large handfuls of sawdust. The hen will generally compact this into the shape she requires for her nest. Some hens delight in throwing out all the sawdust through the entrance hole and it has to be replenished. This seems to be just a playful habit, because once the hen starts laying, she no longer throws out the sawdust.

Sawdust or shavings should never be bought from woodworking shops or timber yards just because it is a little cheaper. Some of the timber may have been treated with preservatives or chemicals which could cause stomach upsets or even be lethal. Mice or rats could have had access either to the wood or to the sawdust or shavings. Although a little more expensive, it is far safer to buy sawdust or shavings that have been sterilised.

NEST FEATHER SHOWS
These shows are usually held by local clubs to enable their members to discover whether they have bred any birds with particular show potential, and also whether their fellow members have had successful breeding seasons. As the name implies, the emphasis at these shows is on the youngsters which still have their first feathers, those with which they left the nest. In the case of the normal varieties they will still be showing their barred heads, and with others the eyes will not yet be showing the white iris rings. Sometimes, with smaller clubs, there will not be sufficient entries to warrant holding a show exclusively for nest feather birds, and they will schedule classes for the older birds too. This happens particularly with cage bird societies which also cater for canaries and other varieties. Newcomers to the hobby, who might wish to exhibit their older birds, should check first with the club as to what classes are being scheduled.

NIGHT FRIGHT
Night fright is certainly an alarming phenomenon to witness. The birds are in a state of absolute panic. They fly into each other, into perches and against walls. Even bright lights have no immediate effect on the obvious terror which collectively grips them. After a while, with full lights on, they begin to calm down and within a short period they are chirping again as if nothing had happened, but during the period of panic they can do themselves considerable physical harm and it can cause untold trouble when nesting hens leave their boxes and fly madly about the breeding cages, sometimes too upset ever to return to their boxes and babies. Every precaution should be taken to prevent night fright ever occurring.

As its name implies, night fright happens during the hours of darkness. The causes are many. Lights flashing into the birdroom, when there are no night lights, can upset the birds. A sudden, unexpected noise, like a dog barking very close to the aviary, can startle them. Animals brushing along the walls of the aviary, or wild animals moving around by night in sight of the birds can frighten them. Overcrowding can mean that the birds have insufficient room to settle and rest. A bird can slip from its perch, or off the wire netting if it has not been able to find a perch. Any of these things can start off the panic which spreads like wildfire.

O

Night lights are of the greatest assistance. By giving a small amount of light, insufficient to disturb the birds, but enough to give a hen, which has left the nest, sufficient light to find her way back, or a bird which has slipped from a perch to find another, they often prevent disaster and, rather like a night light for a child, they instil confidence which prevents fear of the unknown when unexpected noises occur. Care should be taken, when siting an aviary or birdroom, to take account of possible causes of night fright and, if possible, to eliminate them.

NORMALS
Normals is the name given to the budgerigars which were first known, before the many mutations which gave rise to the new varieties. In general they are the green series (green, yellow and grey green) and the blue series (blue, white, violet and grey) which have black spots and markings on the cheeks, back of head, neck and wings.

NOVICE
When the beginner has completed his first three years and has achieved the necessary number of wins, he enters the novice section. If he has not achieved the requisite wins, he may continue to show as a beginner because the rules state that he may remain a beginner 'for three years or a number of wins' (see *BEGINNER*), whichever is the longer period. He is allowed to stay in the novice section for a further three years, or until he has achieved four wins in full classes at open shows. Again, this is whichever is the longer period.

OATS
Oats are a useful supplementary food during the breeding season but care must be taken that the birds are not given these in excess, because they cause obesity if used indiscriminately. They can be fed in a dry state, but are more beneficial to hens rearing chicks if they have been soaked for 24 hours, because the germinating process turns the starch content of the oats into *dextrine* which is an aid to digestion and increases the production of *crop milk*. It is very much appreciated by the birds who would eat far more than they should if given the opportunity. About two teaspoons per pair per day should be given, with a little extra when the chicks are about three weeks old and need more feeding.

The oats should be rinsed first of all to remove any dust and dirt, then covered with hot water and left to soak for twelve hours. The stale water is then thrown away and the oats rinsed through with clean water. They should be covered with cold water and left for a further twelve hours, then given a final rinse. A very useful utensil to use for soaking and rinsing oats or mung beans is the set of plastic buckets described under *EQUIPMENT*. Very occasionally, one comes across a pair of birds which ignore the oats. If there are any oats left over, they should be removed and thrown away after 24 hours, as they may become sour very quickly.

OPALINE
Opaline, a sex-linked mutation, can be introduced into all varieties of budgerigars. It varies from the normal colour by a suffused opalescent effect and the basic colour extending over the top of the head to a point level with the butt of the wings, leaving a clear and distinct V of colour between the wings. This clarity of colour is one

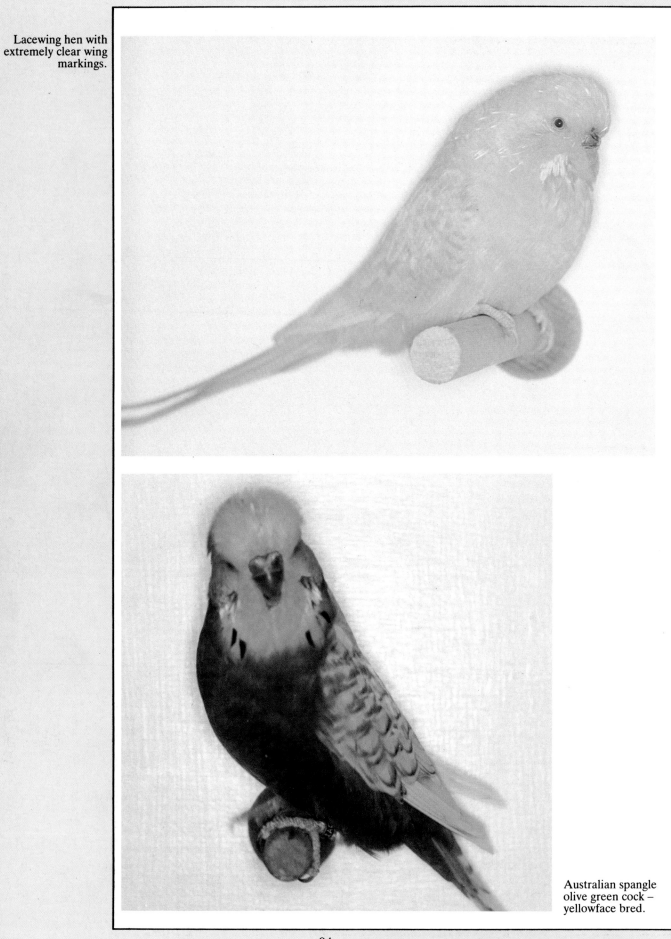

Lacewing hen with extremely clear wing markings.

Australian spangle olive green cock – yellowface bred.

The new varieties

Yellowface cobalt crest cock.

of the features most sought after in an opaline by the show exhibitor.

OPEN SHOWS

As their title implies, these shows are open to any exhibitor, whether or not he is a member of the show-promoting society. Most bird clubs endeavour to hold one of these shows each year, usually commencing the organisation of the next year's show immediately after one has been completed. The size of the show and its entry are a matter of prestige for the club, so they are widely advertised and cash specials and perpetual trophies are offered with a view to attracting entries. Most open shows cater for the four sections, plus classes for juniors, and offer an extensive classification. Entries vary from a few hundred cages to five or six thousand at the Budgerigar Society World Championship. In America classes are smaller because of the vast distances which have to be travelled to shows. In the UK, the majority of open shows are one-day events, with only the major fixtures lasting two days, but in America two days is the normal length of open shows to allow for the competitors staying overnight at the venue. Another great centre for large-entry shows is Germany. Because the German system of judging occupies more time than that of the UK, they seldom stage a one-day event.

Raising funds for the club's prestigious open show is something which occupies the active members for a large part of the year. Prize draws are organised, car boot sales held, bring and buy evenings of items of equipment take place and members donate birds for auction. This usually makes for a social atmosphere at a number of the club's meetings.

It is the aim of most exhibitors to breed a bird which will win at a prestigious show such as the BS World Championship Show. Very many birds, which have carried home the honours, the trophies and prize money at the smaller open shows, are hard-pressed to win even a prize card at the World Championship; in fact, winning a prize card at such a show is considered to be an achievement.

ORIGIN

The origin of *Melopsittacus undulatus*, or as we know it, the budgerigar, seems to have been lost in time. The first picture of the little wild Australian undulated parakeet was published in 1805, but budgerigars were already there in their thousands when the first white settlers arrived on the east coast of the Australian continent. It is generally believed that their name came about when the white settlers asked the Aborigines what they were. Legend has it that the Aborigines repeated again and again something which sounded rather like, betgerrygah, which the settlers later found meant 'good to eat'. By

Part of the show hall at the Budgerigar World Championship Show with over 6,000 exhibits benched.

this time, however, the name had stuck and, with various alterations to allow for regional speech and translation, it eventually became established as budgerigar. In the USA, only the fanciers refer to the birds as budgerigars; the general public still call them parakeets.

OUTCROSSING

Anyone who has embarked on *in-breeding* or *line breeding* will, eventually, need to bring in an out-cross to introduce hybrid vigour and prevent all his own birds from becoming too closely related. The experienced, established breeder will know how to go about this, will know which source of supply would be most beneficial, and which are available. The beginner, or novice, who has begun in-breeding or line breeding without the necessary experience, in the hope that this will quickly improve the quality of his stock, often finds that all that he is doing is multiplying the faults in his stud, and he soon has most of his birds so closely related and his birdroom so full that he has now no possibility of buying in birds with more desirable features. Buying outcrosses without thought can be expensive and time-wasting.

It should be accepted that building up the stock into worthwhile show birds is a slow but sure process. The first task is to study your own birds. Ask the advice of an experienced breeder, and if he tells you that they have a very long way to go before they can be show birds, accept his word. Find out all the faults you should try to eradicate and any good points on which you should build. Write down a list of features where your birds are lacking. Now study the show results in the bird magazines and note down people who consistently win in the breeder classes in the colours or varieties in which you are interested. When you have discovered someone, preferably not too far away, you should arrange a visit to see their birds. This is important, because it does happen that a fancier can have two or three outstanding birds which constantly win, but which have been 'flukes' which will keep him at the top for one season only. If you have access to any older books or magazines, it would be useful to check that the same breeder has been winning in the past, before making your choice. Provided that you see, in the stock of the person you have decided to visit, the main feature you have decided is lacking in your birds, it is then a good idea to try to purchase two of his cocks. It is better to buy cocks than hens, because they are more flexible and, used wisely, they can be bred from for two or three years if they are of good enough quality. Never expect to buy the perfect bird. Unless there is something wrong with it, it is never for sale. It is far better to look for birds that really excel in the one feature you are looking for, providing they have no serious faults.

If the birds available do not have the feature or features you are seeking, don't buy just to be polite; thank the fancier for allowing you to see his birds, but look elsewhere until you find what you are looking for.

The way to implant the genes of your two outcrosses into your stock is to use each cock with two different hens in the first season, then, in the second year of breeding, you select the four best young hens you have bred and breed them back to the cocks which were not their fathers. It is from these pairings that you will begin to see improvement in the feature which was lacking. Each desirable feature is introduced in the same way. Breeding budgerigars is a hobby which requires patience and dedication. It is not for those who imagine they will plunge straight in in the first year and begin to produce perfect birds.

When the first desired feature has been established, it is time to go back to the same source as your first acquisition and purchase further birds with a family relationship to the outcrosses you originally bought. This is known as *controlled outcrossing*. This time you will be buying to eradicate another fault, or to introduce another desired feature. If you bought wisely on the first occasion, you will have implanted genes in your stock which have already improved them. Now you will be adding to these beneficial genes. In time, it will be to your stock that beginners will turn when they want to improve, and if you have been patient and continually tried to upgrade your stud, you will be able to help them.

OVERCROWDING

Overcrowding is possibly the biggest single problem a beginner will have to face and its onset is often not realised until it is too late. The youngsters arrive and suddenly the accommodation available will not stretch to hold the number of birds there now are.

Overcrowding a birdroom or aviary can bring many problems. Fighting occurs as the birds battle for a place to perch. Night disturbance can happen, with all the resulting chaos that that can cause (see *NIGHT FRIGHT*). If any bird becomes sick, there is nowhere it can go for peace and quiet. Many veterinary authorities claim that overcrowding causes *stress* and this can be a killer for birds. If any illness is lying dormant, stress will bring it into an active condition. The birds are irritable, off colour and miserable. On the perching available, every bird should have sufficient room to open its wings, both in the daytime and in the sleeping quarters.

It is so very easy, in a garden aviary, to be kind to your neighbours and callers and accept every stray or unwanted pet, but you will be being very unkind to your birds if this results in overcrowding. It is also very easy to fill every breeding cage you possess without thinking about the number of birds for which you have space in the flights. After a good breeding season, the stock may well have quadrupled and the birds will be grossly overcrowded in the flights and sleeping quarters.

Overcrowding can be prevented by forethought and the breeder owes it to his birds to think carefully and plan any additions to his flock.

Surplus birds can be sold to dealers who advertise in the fancy press.

P

PAIRING

Pairing up your birds is probably the most important time of the year. On this will depend the quantity of youngsters you will produce, for if the birds are not fit when they are paired up, they are unlikely to breed as well as they would if paired up at the height of breeding fitness. On your choice of which cock you will pair with which hen will depend the quality of your stock for the next year and even for years to come.

For the last couple of weeks before the vital day, the cocks and hens should be split into two separate flights.

When you come to do the pairing up, there should be as little distraction as possible. A sensible idea is to prepare the breeding cages a week beforehand so that there is no worry about having to get them done before you can put the birds in. Shavings, or whatever is used for floor covering, seed and grit should all be in place, with fresh water added at the last minute.

The birds do not need to be in perfect feather condition to be ready for breeding, but they must be physically fit and should not be carrying any excess weight. Before being paired up, they should have lost any excess fat which has been put on for showing. Ascertaining breeding condition is not easy for the inexperienced. If the birds are seen making up to one bird while chasing away any others which try to preen or chat with it, it is one sign. Seeing the birds tapping at the perches is another. Seeing cocks and hens trying to feed each other through the wire separating their two flights is a third. It is not necessary for the birds to be flying about madly, but they must be very alert.

All the birds which appear to be in breeding condition, and which you feel have the right potential to be in the breeding team, should be caught up and put into stock cages – cocks and hens separately. After waiting a few days for the birds to settle down and for you to observe them, the best hen should be placed in a show cage. She should be the bird which looks smart, elegant and feminine, a bird that is balanced in all her features, the hen which is the nearest you possess to the written and pictorial representations of the ideal hen. Now you compare this hen with your cocks one by one, always looking for balance, for features which would complement those of the hen. Always watch for obvious faults in either bird. If you are unable to remember these automatically, then write down a list and have it in front of you as you make your choices. Some of the most common faults to watch for are:

> Dropped tail
> Narrow face
> Small head
> Short mask
> Misshapen spots
> Head flecking
> Crossed flights
> Dirty-backed opalines

It is far easier not to use birds with these faults than to try to 'breed them out'. Just keep them flying around for their colour, but don't use them for breeding. They will either reproduce the faults you don't want or, even worse, leave the genes for these faults in your birds in a hidden form, only to come out at a later date.

Never, never put together for breeding two birds carrying the same fault. You will establish a fault which can never be eradicated.

When you have decided which cock you will put with your best hen, you start on the second best hen and so on down the line, always comparing, looking for visual defects and, if you have kept records, checking that none of them are carrying faults you would not want to reproduce.

Pairing up is a long job, particularly if you have a large number of breeding cages and pairs to fill them. If you get tired or irritable, stop for that day and go back to the task fresh another day, otherwise you may be tempted just to put any two birds together to get the task completed. Like sticking a pin in a coupon to find a winner, it very seldom works.

PARASITES

The parasites most likely to infest budgerigars are *lice, mite* and *worms*. Lice have a flat form and can lie very close to the skin. They lay tacky, triangular eggs, or nits, which cling to the feathers and hatch within a few weeks of being laid. They multiply so quickly that one pair can produce 100,000 descendants in roughly three months. Overcrowding, where the birds are huddled together, can lead to an explosion of the louse population. They live on the surface layers of skin and some, the *depluming lice*, actually bite at the growing feathers. They cause intense irritation to the birds and should be avoided or eradicated. If it is found that the birds are affected by lice, they should be washed in a solution of warm soapy water to which a pyrethrum solution has been added and then sprayed with a pyrethrum dusting powder. The birdroom, perches, breeding cages, nesting boxes, or whatever else the birds have been in contact with, should be thoroughly washed, disinfected and sprayed with an anti-mite or anti-lice solution.

Mite vary in size between $\frac{1}{10}$-$\frac{9}{10}$ mm in length and are barely visible to the naked eye unless they are moving against a contrasting coloured background, or if they are in large numbers, or engorged with blood. Those most likely to affect budgerigars have been described under *MITE* and *SCALY FACE*.

Worms are passed through eggs laid in the faeces of a bird. Very often they are introduced through droppings of wild birds landing in the outside flights. The eggs develop into larvae which are swallowed by the budgerigars when they peck around on the floor. They can remain alive outside a host body for up to three months. Once inside the body, they develop and can cause debility and loss of condition quite quickly. The worms can also become impacted and block the small intestine. This can cause a *paralysis* of the legs as well as acute discomfort to the bird.

Varieties of feather mite.

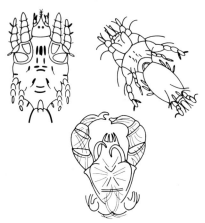

To relieve the discomfort and apparent paralysis, a little liquid paraffin should be administered. It is possible to introduce this into the beak with a small pipette, or on the end of a piece of millet spray stalk. Just get one drop into the beak, wait until the bird has swallowed it and repeat the dose. This should be repeated daily until the worms have been passed. They can be seen in the droppings, sometimes even with the naked eye. They are whitish, round and a little smaller than pinheads. The really ideal way to worm a bird is with a stomach tube, because this ensures that the worm cure is swallowed in its entirety, but there are several difficulties for the breeder who wants to attempt this task himself. A thin plastic tube is put onto the end of a hypodermic syringe and is fed down the back of the throat into the crop, and the treatment then pumped in from the syringe. The safest drug for this is Panacure, obtainable from a veterinary surgeon who will also work out the correct dose. Before the tube is fed down into the throat, it should be lubricated with a little liquid paraffin. The difficulties which can be experienced are that the bird has a strong beak and could, and often does, bite off the plastic tube. Another trouble is that it is possible for the inexperienced person to feed the tube down the windpipe instead of into the crop, and if anything was then pumped down, it would cause immediate asphyxiation.

A third method of worming is to add Nemicide or Lethomycil combined with glucose (they are both very bitter) to the water supply. The difficulty here is that it is not possible to know if the bird has drunk the correct dose. No water should be given to the bird or birds – many authorities suggest that all the stock should be treated as a precaution – for 24 hours before treatment so that they will be thirsty. Your veterinarian will work out the dosage in accordance with the average weight of the birds and the number to be treated.

If a pet bird is suspected of having worms, or if they have been seen in the droppings, the owner should take it to a vet immediately and not attempt to treat it himself. Worms are not prevalent in budgerigar flocks and most fanciers are never faced with this problem, therefore worming is not carried out widely.

PARTNERSHIPS
In budgerigar shows, two or more breeders may, if they wish, show as partners. This method is often used by close friends or relatives who do not wish to compete against each other. More than two people may exhibit as partners and partnerships of up to four are known. Partnerships can often be matters of convenience. One partner takes the birds to a show one week and another the next. Each looks after the other's birds when he or she is on holiday. The Budgerigar Society subscription for partnerships is the same as if each is a single member, and there are rules which must be followed. In the first year a partnership is formed, they may show birds in breeders' classes wearing any one of the partnership's ring numbers, but in subsequent years one ring number is normally allocated by the BS office, which they must all use to allow them to exhibit their young stock.

PATRONAGE
When a society or club donates rosettes, cash, plaques or other prizes to another society's show, it

is said to have granted it patronage. This is a very widespread procedure throughout the fancy. Small clubs grant patronage to their neighbours or their area society with the stipulation that only their own members may win the awards. In this way they hope to increase their membership. Area societies grant patronage to all their affiliated societies in the hope of gaining both new affiliated societies and new members for themselves. The Budgerigar Society grants a huge list of patronages throughout the country. These are granted at different levels according to the size of the shows. Among the items they donate are the highly prestigious *challenge certificates* which are awarded to shows of championship status. Most of the larger clubs are prepared to offer a large number of perpetual trophies and cash prizes at their shows to ensure that they receive sufficient entries to qualify for championship status.

Budgerigar Society patronage is very much welcomed by overseas societies and is granted to many major events. In return, these societies offer their rosettes for competition at the BS Club Show. Patronage is also exchanged between major clubs in many countries, particularly for silver or golden jubilee events.

PERCHES

In the flights, perches should be substantial and secure as there will be a number of birds, all bent on destruction, gnawing away at them. The most sensible size for the perches is 5 x 2.5 cm (2 x 1 in) timber and they should be fixed so that they will be perfectly steady even when a number of birds all alight on them at the same time. They should be positioned to allow the maximum flying space for the birds and at least one of the sets of perches should be placed under an area of solid roofing to enable the birds to shelter from the elements, be it hot sun or driving rain. Branches of trees make very good perches, and very good playgrounds for budgerigars. They will strip the branches of leaves and bark, so it is essential that no branches of laburnum, or other poisonous trees, are used. Apple, pear and plum trees are the most popular for this purpose.

In the breeding cages, hardwood dowelling 1.25 or 1.5 cm (½ or ⅝ in) diameter can be used, but the surface does become slippery and the birds, therefore, may have difficulty in gripping the perch. This can cause problems during mating when the hen requires a firm grip. Another disadvantage of round or oval dowel perches is that the birds' toes are kept permanently curled in

An arrangement of perches.

one position, which can cause corns to form. It is far better to make the perches from 2 x 1.5 cm (¾ x ⅝ in) softwood. These are cut about 2.5 cm (1 in) longer than the depth of the breeding cage. A thin nail, or a panel pin, is driven into one end. A hole is drilled into the back wall of the cage at the height and position you want the perch, on a level with a cross wire. The perch is pushed through the wire front, aiming the pin towards the back of the cage. The pin is slotted into the hole at the back and the front pressed down until it fits tightly on the cross wire.

In a pet cage, it is advantageous to replace one of the round perches with a square one made from softwood. This allows the bird a change of position for its toes and is so cheap that it can be renewed at any time when the playful little creature decides to gnaw through it.

The round, sanded tubes sold to cover perches are not a good idea. They are not firm which causes the bird to wobble when it lands, and they are very rough for tender young feet to land and stand on. Corns and bleeding feet have been caused by these tubes.

PETS

Budgerigars make ideal pets for many reasons. They are usually allowed even when the landlord's rule is 'no pets'. Children who long for a pet, but have allergies to the fur of dogs or cats, can very often tolerate budgies. Older people find them wonderful company, while they do not need to be taken for walks and are quite capable of providing their own exercise. It is far easier to find someone who is prepared to take a budgie as a 'house guest' while the family are on holiday, than to find someone willing to accept a pet with more demands. They are affectionate, amusing and colourful and, provided that their owner has patience, they can learn to talk. Given all these advantages, they are also very cheap to keep. Their requirements are very modest – clean seed, a little grit, and the odd piece of fruit or greenfood and they will stay happy and healthy.

Doctors have stated that owning a budgerigar or budgerigars has great therapeutic value for anyone confined to a house on their own. They provide companionship and are 'someone to talk to'. Aviaries or stock cages of budgerigars have been set up in many old people's homes, in long-term hospital wards and even in prisons – on doctors' orders.

One of the strangest stories of budgies as a form of therapeutic benefit comes from Broadmoor Prison for the criminally insane. A humane and understanding superintendent, back in 1956, gave permission to a patient to build and stock an aviary. Other patients came to see the birds and were fascinated. The hobby snowballed; everyone wanted budgies. The doctors and staff found them to be of such great value in keeping the patients occupied, happy and healthy that permission was given for anyone who wanted to have breeding units fitted in their wards. Broadmoor blossomed with budgies. They were in wards, galleries, day rooms, they flew free in corridors and a budgie and bird club was organised by one of the inmates who became its first chairman, while another acted as secretary. They corresponded with bird clubs on the 'outside', and received many visits from speakers of repute from all over the country.

Budgerigars can be very affectionate pets that may even become friendly with other members of the household, but never take a chance like this!

Eventually the patient fancier was released and slowly the enthusiasm for budgies waned. That same patient is now back in Park Lane Hospital, Liverpool and is doing everything in his power to obtain permission to breed budgies and form a club there.

PIED FACTOR

The pied factor modifies the normal variety by adding certain variations to the colouring. There are three types of pieds, the *dominant* pied, the *recessive* pied and the *clearflight*. As its name implies, the dominant pied cannot be carried in a recessive or split form. If it is there, it is visible. The general body colour is that of the normal variety, except that it has irregular patches of yellow on the green series, or white on the blue series, or it can have a clear band of the colour, about 1.25 cm (½ in) wide, around the middle of the body. The wings, again, are similar to those of the normal, except for irregular patches of clear colour and clear flight feathers.

The *recessive* pied is considered to be one of the most colourful of all the many varieties of budgerigars and is a great favourite as a pet. Unfortunately, until recently, the breeders of this variety have not been able to improve the size of the bird up to that of the normal or the dominant pied varieties, which has made it rather unpopular as a show bird. The general colour of the body of the light green bird is a series of irregular patches of clear yellow and bright grass green, the flight feathers are usually of clear buttercup yellow and the wings are mainly clear with a few black undulations or polka dots. In the blue series, white replaces yellow and blue replaces green. One of the loveliest combinations is the violet and white of the violet recessive pied. It is not a fault in show birds if the full complement of spots is not carried.

The *clearflight* is another dominant variety. The general body colour is that of the normal variety, except for a small patch on the top of the head, about the size of a thumbnail, which is clear yellow in the green series or clear white in the blues. The wings are similar to those of the normals, except that seven flight feathers must be visible, and they and the tail must be of pure yellow on green, or pure white on blue. Dark feathers in the flights constitute a fault for exhibition purposes.

PIN FEATHERS

The term pin feathers or pen feathers is given to newly growing feathers, particularly on the top of the head, that have not yet broken through and discarded their quills. As these spoil the appearance of the bird for show purposes, many fanciers attempt to speed up the opening of these feathers. The method used is to wash the head in warm water each day for a few days before a show, using an old, soft toothbrush and always brushing in the direction the feathers are growing. This helps to loosen the quill and allows the feather to spread out naturally. Quite often, one bird will pick away the quills on top of another's head, because it is the one spot where the bird cannot reach to clear away the quill itself.

PROTECTION

Only you can protect your birds from the many harmful possibilities they may have to face. Hygiene and cleanliness are two items which only you can provide. They need

Budgerigars are inquisitive pets who love to sample their owners' food and drink. Do not let them try anything hot and spicy.

protection from vermin and from hot sun, winds and rain – see *BIRDROOMS*. Flashing lights or strange noises at night can cause havoc – see *NIGHT FRIGHT*.

In the home, fires need to be covered before a bird is allowed out of its cage. A bird doesn't understand that there is glass in a window and can do itself harm by flying madly into the window pane until it realises it is there. Curtains should be closed until the bird is used to the room. Doors should always be kept closed when a bird is flying free. Cats, and sometimes dogs, should be kept away from the free bird, or from the cage where they could cause stress and frighten the occupant nearly to death.

Whatever the danger, the birds must be able to rely on you for protection. It is you who must foresee any hazard – and make sure it is removed.

PROTEINS

Proteins are long chains of *amino acids* used in the formation of body tissues needed for growth and for the formation of eggs. For this reason it is necessary to supply some form of additional *protein* to the birds when they are breeding and feeding babies, because seed does not supply all the protein which is needed at this time. Chicken's eggs are a very good source of protein and are readily accepted by the breeding pairs when mixed in their softfood. Other sources of animal protein are meat, cheese, milk and fish. Some fanciers keep bones from meat, carcasses of chickens and even fish and fish roe to feed to their birds and claim to have excellent results. Others substitute milk, or half-milk and half-water for the normal water supply. If any of these food supplements are given, it is vitally important that they are fresh and that any not eaten the same day are removed, because these animal proteins can be a source of *salmonella* bacteria which can cause many of the gut diseases. Plant proteins are often deficient in some of the necessary amino acids, which is why the supplementary protein is necessary at breeding time, although

at all times the bird is using protein to build feathers and replace any body tissues broken down in bodily functions.

Protein is the last storehouse of energy the bird possesses. If it is starved of necessities, it uses up all the excess fat it has stored in its tissues. Only when that is completely depleted does it start using up its stores of protein. Muscle wastage ensues, the flesh over the breastbone disappears, waste products accumulate in the body and often gouty deposits affect the joints of the limbs. Unless protein is provided regularly, the bird will die. This condition can happen when a bird of either sex is attempting to rear too many chicks and is so conscientious that it forgets to eat sufficient to supply its own needs as well as those of the chicks.

R

RARE VARIETIES

A specialist society exists in the UK for birds designated as rare varieties and colours, and the birds so covered change from time to time as a variety becomes more common or as a new mutation appears. In other countries, the 'rares' can be of different varieties, because some which are popular in one country can be almost unobtainable in another. Those considered to be rare at the present moment in Britain are the following: English fallows which have solid red eyes, and German fallows which have a white iris ring (both are recessive varieties); lacewings which also have the white iris ring and are very similar in appearance to the fallows; clearflights, one of the pied varieties, which is dominant; light yellow and whites of light suffusion and olive yellow (all are recessive to normals, clearwings and greywings); slates, a very rare variety, hardly ever seen nowadays and sex-linked; clearbodies and brownwings which are listed by the 'rares' society although at the moment none are known in the UK; greywings which are seen occasionally (they are dominant to clearwings, yellows and white but recessive to the normal varieties); and finally the two double dark colours of the green and blue series, that is the olives and mauves.

RECESSIVE FACTORS

Budgerigars can appear to be of one colour while carrying a gene for a completely different colour and this can cause a great deal of confusion among beginners. For instance, they may pair together two visually green birds and produce youngsters which are all blue. They are surprised and uncertain why this has occurred. The reason is that both the parents have been bred from a bird carrying a blue gene. Some time in the past, one of their ancestors was the result of a pairing of one green bird and one blue bird. Green being dominant to blue, the resulting chicks would all be green and it is possible that, through several generations, those birds have always been mated with green birds. However, that blue gene would still remain, recessive, unseen, but still there. Then one day, the two greens, both carrying the recessive blue gene, are paired together and fate decrees that the two blue genes join together in each egg. Each time this happens, a blue bird is produced. As green is dominant, it would show if it was present, therefore these blue birds are not split for green, and when bred with other blues will produce only blues – unless the other blues are, in turn, split for white which is the recessive form of blue. If two blue birds, both with ancestors which were white, should join together, then white birds could be produced.

Colour is just one of the recessive factors; many more exist which carry such faults as *dropped tail*, excess *melanin* which causes flecking on the head, the *dirty backs* which are displayed by some opalines, or perhaps some for feather texture, spots and any other feature. Not enough is known about how these features are carried and whether they are dominant or recessive. Those people who have tried to work out the genes carrying, say, feather texture have admitted defeat; they have been unable to plot the pattern. With computers now being used to store genetical breeding records, it is hoped that eventually someone will invent tables of inheritance in the same way that Dr Duncker was able to do with the colours.

RECORDS

Accurate practical records are essential for the serious budgerigar breeder. The first necessity is the nest record card. On this is recorded the colour of the cock and hen and their ring numbers, the date they are paired and the number of the cage they will occupy. It will usually be found that, over the years, a certain cage, or batch of cages, is more successful than others. It is important to find out the reason for this. Is an unsuccessful cage situated too low? Is it in a corner and too dark? Is it directly in front of a light and therefore too light? There is always a reason and the successful breeder can rectify faults in positioning from a careful study of his records.

As the breeding cycle progresses, the date the first egg is laid is recorded, and also the date it is due to hatch, the date each chick is actually hatched and then which ring number has been given to it. It is wise to add such items as troubles with feeding, feather plucking, or any other information which you feel will be of use to you in the future.

When time permits, or at the end of the breeding season, all the details on the nest record cards should be transferred into the breeding register. This is a master record of all the nest record cards. The more information which can be recorded in this book, the better. Memories are short and some of the details about the behaviour of the pair might be vital in the following year's breeding season. It is very important to write down every major fault which might occur in order to be forewarned. The wise breeder records everything which might guide him in future plans, i.e.:

1 Are the hens good feeders and from a family of good feeders?
2 Are the hens from a highly fertile family?
3 What sort of mortality rate is there in the offspring from this pair and what is the history of mortality in the family?
4 Has the family a history of longevity?
5 Are there any family illnesses or weaknesses?
6 Is the family slow to mature?
7 Is the family strong for quality in cocks or hens?
8 Is the family strong for quantity of cocks or of hens?

All these points are important for the fancier who hopes to succeed.

Every breeding register needs a section of *stock records*. This will tell you whether a bird has been retained for future breeding or for showing, whether it was sold or whether it died. If a pattern of high death rate emerges in a particular family, it must be investigated and the cause discovered if possible. If it is found that the offspring from one particular family is always among the birds which were sold over the years, then it becomes obvious that the standard of this family is not up to your own requirement and it may be wiser to dispose of the whole family and concentrate on those which are consistently giving better results.

The more records you keep, the more you learn about your birds and the better able you are to steer the stud into the top winning stream. A *show register* is not really essential but is very helpful for beginners. The name and date of a show is entered, together with your list of entries. When the results are known, successes and failures are recorded, together with the number of entries in each class. To enter 'first' against a bird means nothing unless the number of birds in the class is also entered; it does not help to know that three firsts were gained if there was only one bird in each of the classes. A very important point to note is the name of the judge who was engaged for the show. Every judge is different and sees the birds in his own way. They all have preferences and it is a wise exhibitor who studies these. Although they all judge to the one standard for condition, deportment, size, etc., one may consider a grubby back on an opaline to be the *most* undesirable fault in a budgerigar, while another considers that the overall impression of the bird is more important than its markings. The beginner who studies the judges under whom he shows, often makes greater progress than one who believes that every judge should have the same preference that he has.

RED MITE
This subject has been fully dealt with under *MITE*.

REGURGITATION

This perfectly natural habit of budgerigars often distresses owners of pet birds or beginner breeders. The budgerigar feeds its young by first dehusking the seed, partially digesting it and then regurgitating the partially digested food and feeding it direct into the beak of the baby. This is also done as a mark of affection; in this way the cock feeds the hen with whom he would choose to mate if he was given a free choice. Fortunately, the desire to mate and reproduce is very strong and affairs in the flight are very soon forgotten when your chosen cock and hen are confined together in the breeding cage and he settles down to feed first her and then the chicks. A pet bird will accept a mirror as a substitute companion and 'feed' the mirror until it is covered and no longer reflects the image companion. Even the babies will attempt to feed each other when they first emerge from the nest box.

Those who have studied the nesting habits of budgerigars in the wild in Australia report that the hen lays the clutch at the bottom of a hole in a hollow tree, sometimes several feet from the entrance. The cock forages for seeding grasses, insects and other food with which to feed her and brings it back to the nest. He regurgitates it for the hen and, in turn, she regurgitates the food again to feed the babies. When the first baby is about three weeks old, the hen flies off to find another nest and the oldest chick is left to climb up the tree trunk, meet the cock who has been finding food, and then transfer it down to the younger chicks still at the bottom of the hole. When the oldest one is ready to fly away, the second son or daughter takes on the feeding duties and so on, until the final one has flown. From this, it is obvious that regurgitation is a part and parcel of normal behaviour. It should not, however, be confused with *vomiting*. In budgerigars this is violent and the birds appear distressed. It has been dealt with under *AILMENTS* and *DISEASES*.

RINGS

Closed coded rings are a permanent means of identifying a bird. The ring is made from dyed aluminium and the colour changes each year, therefore it is possible to look at birds flying around with, say, purple rings on their legs and immediately identify them as having been hatched in 1987. The rings are issued by the ruling body in most countries where budgerigars are bred and exhibited. In the UK this is the Budgerigar Society. The year of issue, followed by the serial number of the bird and then the code number of the breeder is stamped on each one.

Split rings, as their name implies, can be opened and therefore can be placed on the bird's leg when it is an adult. They can be obtained in most colours, or in a combination of colours, and are used to identify

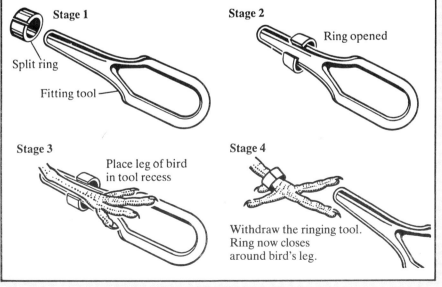

Stage 1
Split ring
Fitting tool

Stage 2
Ring opened

Stage 3
Place leg of bird in tool recess

Stage 4
Withdraw the ringing tool. Ring now closes around bird's leg.

Fitting a split ring on the leg of a budgerigar.

families. When a breeder specialises in a certain colour, say blue, he might have a flight full of blue birds and have difficulty in identifying individual birds. By using a distinctive coloured split ring for each different family, he can immediately pick out related birds.

Although split rings can be put on the leg at any age of a bird's life, if they are being used for the purpose of identifying a family, they are best put on before the young are taken away from their parents. It is a simple task as, when the rings are bought, a ringing tool is supplied. The ring is slipped onto the tool with the split in line with the groove, the leg of the bird is laid in the tool and the tool is then withdrawn along the leg, leaving the ring attached. If the ring has not quite closed up tightly after being stretched, it can be closed quite easily with thumb and finger.

RINGING A CHICK

The *closed coded ring* should be placed on the bird's leg when it is between five and ten days old. It is better to put the ring on early and risk having it come off and need to be put on again; than to leave it until the foot is too big for the ring to slip over and thus to risk hurting the chick.

It is important that your hands are kept warm when ringing chicks because they have been taken from beneath a warm hen in a warm nest box and the shock of being held in freezing cold hands could be fatal. Those who suffer from cold hands should have hot water, a hot radiator or even a hot water bottle available for warming their hands before beginning to carry out the task of ringing chicks.

The operation of ringing a chick can be quite frightening to a raw beginner. It is worth while practising

Two methods of ringing a chick; with two toes facing forward and two facing back: or with three facing forward and one facing back.

1. The two forward, two back method.

a) Place ring over two front toes.

b) Pull the long rear toe through with a toothpick or pointed matchstick.

c) Pull short rear toe through leaving ring just above ankle joint.

d) Ring in position.

2. The three forward method.

a) Gather the three long toes together.

b) Place ring over three long toes and gently push ring over ball of foot.

c) Carefully pull the short toe through to clear the ring.

d) Ring in position.

at first on a chick whose legs are too small to hold a ring. The ring will slide on easily and can be gently pulled off again without causing any damage or pain to the little baby bird.

There are two methods of ringing a bird in current use. The first is to take the two toes which face forward, place the ring over these and carry on until the ring is over the first joint, then, with an instrument with a blunt point, such as the end part of a small plastic knitting needle, a blunted toothpick or a used match with the head removed and the end cut into a point; first pull the large back toe through the ring, followed by the smaller back toe. The ring will then be positioned on the leg above the first joint.

The second method is to hold the two forward-facing toes and the small backward-facing toe together, place the ring over all three, and then over the first joint. As described above, the one large backward-facing toe is then pulled through the ring with the blunt-pointed instrument. At this age the feet have not properly formed and holding a toe in the wrong direction is not painful or harmful, but remember that they are tender little things, the skin is soft, and gentleness is very important.

ROSETTES

Rosettes come in all shapes and sizes. Some are given by the show-promoting society to the winners of the various sections or to winners of breeder classes, or for winners of classes for specific varieties. Some are patronage rosettes which are donated by outside societies for competition among their own members, and some are donated by overseas societies. They range from a centre marked 'special' and a single frill of ribbon around it, to massive concoctions of row after row of pleated ribbons. The American rosettes are usually the largest and most colourful and are highly prized by their winners.

RULES

Many rules have been formulated by the executive bodies of the budgerigar fancy throughout the world. There are rules which judges must follow, show rules with which exhibitors must comply, rules which must be followed by every member of the society. All these rules have been applied in an attempt to ensure that all exhibitors are given a fair chance at shows and that no one can gain an advantage by dubious practices between shows. The rules differ slightly in different countries and any breeder who moves to another country, or is invited to judge overseas shows, would be wise to study the rules of that country's ruling body.

General rules are basically guidelines for the way the society should be managed and to identify the responsibilities of officials and committees. Specific rules give the procedure to be followed should one member wish to complain about the

actions of another in the unhappy situation that he feels the other has broken the show rules or has in some way strayed from the straight and narrow path of the fancy.

These rules are never intended to be obstructive and, in the UK, have evolved for the betterment of the fancy for over 60 years. Some of the rules of the early years would appear Draconian in this day and age.

Rosettes for a champion breeder.

S

SAFETY DOOR

Fitting a safety door is a simple, straightforward task, but it is a real necessity to avoid losing birds. If doors of breeding cages or the inside flights have been inadvertently left open, or if the young birds pick away at the door fasteners until they succeed in opening them – and this does happen – birds could be flying around when the main door is opened. If a safety door is fitted, there is no danger of them flying straight out.

A frame should be made, the same size as the main door, but opening inwards (provided that the main door opens outwards). As an extra precaution against mice, the lower part of the safety door is covered by a solid material – wood, plastic or metal. The door is then fixed on hinges. It is as simple as that, but it can prevent so much distress.

SAFETY PORCH

A safety porch consists of a metal or timber frame, covered with weldmesh, extending from the entrance door to the birdroom. It is sensible to make it sufficiently large for two people to be able to enter and close the outer porch door before the birdroom door is opened. It would be beneficial to cover the top with some stiff material which will not flap or rattle in the wind because this could disturb the birds. This cover is purely for the breeder's own comfort, so that in wet or inclement weather he is under a roof while locking and unlocking the birdroom door.

Some ready-made birdrooms are constructed in such a way that it is necessary to enter the flight before reaching the sleeping quarters. In this case, the safety porch needs to be at the entry to the flights. The same method as above can be used, except that safety would be improved if the door was no higher than 1.25 m (4 ft). The birds, who normally fly high, would be far less likely to attempt to fly into the safety porch when the flight door is opened if they had to fly downwards towards it.

The weldmesh or any wire netting should be painted with black bitumastic paint, inside and out, to preserve it. This is best applied with a roller.

SCALE OF POINTS

Each country allocates points to the various features of a budgerigar and in some they are still judged on a points system, each feature being considered one at a time and the requisite number of points awarded. All the points awarded for the features are then added and the bird gaining the greatest number is declared the winner of that particular class or section. This method is extremely slow and can only be used where shows are spread over a number of days, or where the number of birds at a show is few. In Britain, with its large shows of up to 6,000 budgerigar entries, it would not be feasible to consider each bird for each aspect, and an overall decision is made by the judges. The judges are, however, all fully conversant with the Budgerigar Society's official scale of points and take them into account in all their deliberations.

For by far the largest number of colours and varieties, the points awarded are:

> 45 for size, shape, balance and deportment;
> 20 for size and shape of head;
> 15 for colour;
> 15 for mask and spots; and
> 5 for wing markings.

In varieties which do not show wing markings, or mask and spots, such as lutinos, clearwings and yellows, the points awarded for these features are added to those allocated for colour. The recessive pied variety, which does not always show the six spots, and, in fact, occasionally has no visible spots, has the 15 points normally allowed for mask and spots added to those awarded for wing markings.

Committees sit for many hours

discussing any changes before the scale of points is ever altered, but occasionally either a colour variety changes to a certain degree, or fashions change, and what was considered to be nearest to the ideal standard at one time is abandoned by the fancy at another. In cases such as these, it is usual for a smaller committee to deliberate and report their findings to the main body before any change is agreed. When changes are made – which is seldom – the whole membership, and the fancy in general, are informed before they are put into operation.

SCALY FACE (or SCALY LEG)

The mite which causes scaly face in birds is related to the same mite which is responsible for *scabies* in humans or *mange* in dogs and cats. They are usually introduced by wild birds alighting on the wires of the flights or, of course, by new acquisitions being introduced into the stud. The birds should always be watched for any sign of scaly face, for if these tiny mites are allowed to breed unchecked, they can cause permanent and irrevocable damage to the beak and/or legs of the bird. The mites actually burrow into the beak, creating thousands of tiny tunnels. The surface appears scaly or crusty for two reasons. First, the irritation causes the bird to exude a sticky liquid, and, second, the mite throw up skin debris when burrowing through skin and beak. Together these two substances produce the dry, chalky substance which we call *scale*. In the majority of cases this is confined to the area around the beak, with the eyes also sometimes being affected. If the first signs of the infestation have not been noticed, the condition later spreads to the legs. In really severe cases, the scale develops into strange horn-like growths, giving the bird a most grotesque appearance.

At the first sign of any scale appearing around the beak, the bird should be isolated and the affected area smeared with sulphur ointment, or Vaseline, every other day for ten days, or until every sign of encrustation has disappeared. Even if no sign is seen on the legs of affected birds, it is as well to smear a little of the ointment over the legs and feet. It will not harm the bird and will ensure that the mites do not move from what will now be an uncomfortable place to one which allows them more freedom. The ointment acts by sealing up the minute holes which have been burrowed, cutting off the air supply and literally asphyxiating the mites.

To clear the birdroom of these mites, the birds should be treated with a safe pyrethrum powder and the birdroom, or breeding cage or cages which have been affected, should be sprayed with a liquid containing an anti-mite preparation.

Sometimes, a pet bird which has not been in contact with other domestic birds or wild birds will suddenly show signs of scaly face. This is a mystery which has not yet been solved satisfactorily. It may have been a mild, lifelong infestation which until now caused no outward signs, or it could have been infestation of the seed bought at a shop where it was kept in close proximity to birds. The reason may never be known, but the treatment is the same. In this case, the cage should be completely immersed in a bath of hot water treated with disinfectant and anti-mite solution, to ensure there will be no repetition

A bird that is suffering from scaly face should be treated regularly until every trace of encrustation has disappeared.

of the condition once the bird has been cleared.

The most common method of transmission of scaly face mite is from parent to offspring during feeding. For this reason, careful check should be kept on the beaks and legs of chicks. Sometimes malformation of the beak can occur in the nestlings and the inexperienced breeder may blame this on a congenital defect, whereas it could have been prevented had treatment been carried out in time.

SEEDS

Because seeds are the most important, and by far the largest, part of the diet of a budgerigar, it is important that the seed should be fresh and of the best quality available. Saving a few pounds on a hundredweight of seed is not nearly so important as keeping the stock fit, active and in top breeding condition. It takes experience to judge the quality of seed by its visual appearance, but by plunging your hand into the sack, it is possible to discover if it is clean or excessively dusty and dirty. Some of the world's most experienced fanciers check the seed by chewing a few grains which should taste sweet and fresh. Testing the seed for fertility is a good indication of its quality too. If 100 seeds are placed between two pieces of damp blotting paper, or thick material, and then kept damp for five days, a number of those seeds should germinate. If less than 65 of the seeds start to grow, then the quality and freshness of the seed is suspect.

Where a large number of birds are kept, it is advisable to feed canary seed separately from the mixed millets and allow the birds to choose for themselves which they will eat. Their choice will differ from season to season.

Canary seed contains approximately 13.5 per cent protein, 4.9 per cent fats or oil, 51 per cent carbohydrates and 2.1 per cent salts and minerals, while millets have a far larger percentage of carbohydrates (60 per cent) and less protein (11.3 per cent). The birds seem to know when they need to eat more millet for fat-producing or heat-producing carbohydrates, and when they need more proteins from the canary seed for body building, feather building and breeding.

Care must be taken in storing seed. If sacks are stored, it is best to keep them off the floor and whatever is used to support them should preferably be plastic or, alternatively, be wrapped in polythene, because no vermin could climb up the smooth surface. If possible the seed should be kept in plastic containers with lids. Seed must never be allowed to become damp as this could cause moulds to form and it has been found that some moulds produce a poison which cannot be eradicated even if the mould later disappears. Mould is also dangerous because it can waft through the air and settle in the air sacs of the birds' lungs.

For the pet cage, many excellent packet seeds are available. These often contain all the requirements for health, including seeds which have been impregnated with vitamins. If seed is bought loose from pet shops, the same precautions must be taken as advised for bulk buying. Check that the sacks are not left where they could be fouled by the droppings of rats or mice, and that they are kept dry. When the seed is kept in the home, an airtight tin or jar is the best type of container to use.

SEED HOPPERS

Seed hoppers come in various shapes and sizes; some are home-made and others can be purchased. The number of birds kept and the size of the flights will influence the type to be chosen.

One which is suitable for the smaller aviary is a large jar or container with outlets so that the seed can fall into a tray which is raised in the centre. It is useful to place a cone on top of the jar. This prevents the birds from landing on the top and so minimises the amount of droppings which can get into the seed.

The wall-mounted hopper is one in popular use. It consists of a container with a number of outlets

An ingenious, but easily constructed seed hopper.

from which the seed falls into a trough. The birds eat the seed and the husks fall away.

The simplest type for large aviaries is a plastic bucket with a section of the bottom cut away. A sloping sheet of a stiff material is inserted into the bucket and allowed to protrude from the bottom. The seed then runs out into a large open dish or tray. When the birds fly down to feed, or up again, their wing action blows away all the husks. This seed hopper is simple, effective and capacious.

Pet birds seldom need seed hoppers, as their seed consumption is so low and can be checked daily. One word of warning: plastic drinking fountains are sometimes used as seed containers or hoppers, particularly by houseproud owners who believe they will prevent seed being scattered. These can be dangerous because the outlet, while suitable for water is not really wide enough to ensure a continuous

supply of seed. Very often these clog up, and while the owner believes that the bird has a full fountain of seed, in reality it has eaten the tiny supply held in the mouth of the hopper and is literally being starved. If the blockage is not noticed, the bird can starve to death in a very short time. It is far better to have a little seed or husks to vacuum and a happy healthy budgerigar.

SEEDING GRASSES
Budgies love seeding grasses, both to play with and to eat. If hung up in the flight, they will be quickly stripped of seeds and greenstuff until all that is left is a bunch of dry stalks. The danger with feeding any wild food nowadays is the many toxic sprays used to keep weeds under control or, strangely enough, even some sprays meant to increase the yield, which would be dangerous if eaten by our birds. Only if the breeder is absolutely sure that the grasses have not been treated in any

Three types of seed hopper.

Opaline skyblue
dominant pied cock

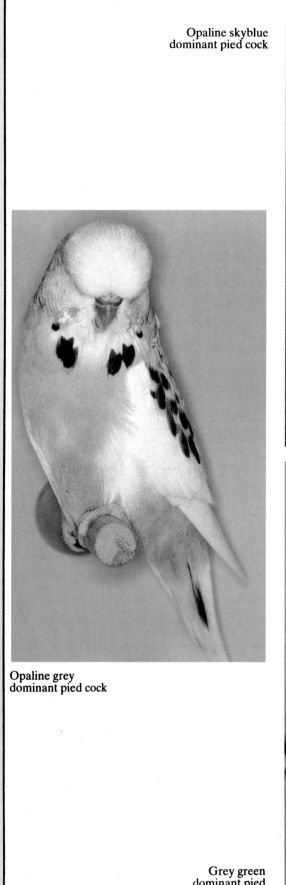

Opaline grey
dominant pied cock

Grey green
dominant pied
cock.

114

Dominant pieds

A delightfully
feminine opaline
cinnamon grey
dominant pied hen

way, and that they could not have been fouled by animals or exhaust fumes, should they be used. Even then, they should be well washed before being offered to the birds. The birds will enjoy them more if they are wet, and use them as a bath to roll about in.

SEX LINKAGE

A variety is described as sex-linked when the gene for that variety is attached to the X, or cock's chromosome. The cock can carry one or two potentials for the variety on its two X chromosomes. If we take cinnamon as an example of these sex-linked varieties, we find that if a cock is carrying two potentials, then it will be a visual cinnamon; if it is carrying one potential, then it will be split for cinnamon, but the cinnamon will not be visible.

The hens have only one X chromosome. If the cinnamon potential has attached itself to that single X chromosome, then the hen is a cinnamon and it is impossible for it to attach itself to the Y, or female, chromosome because it is always linked with the X or male chromosome. For this reason, it is not possible for a hen to carry in a hidden form, or be split for, a sex-linked variety. The six sex-linked varieties are opaline, cinnamon, slate, lacewing, lutino and albino.

SEXING

Sexing budgerigars is generally very easy. The *cere* of the cock is blue and that of the hen brown. Sometimes, however, if either bird is off colour, the ceres become very pale and pasty coloured, particularly that of the hen. Very occasionally a bird can have an apparent *sex change*, the cock's cere becoming a dark chocolate brown. When this happens it is usually possible to see blue underneath the brown, around the edges of the cere. The cere can change back again to blue, but it has been found that such cocks are seldom fertile once this change has occurred.

Sexing can be more difficult with some varieties, such as lutinos and albinos. The adult cocks have a pinky tinge on their pale blue ceres and the hens have pinky fawn coloured ceres which can be quite confusing to breeders not conversant with the *ino varieties*.

When youngsters first leave the nest, the distinction in the colour of ceres is so slight that even very experienced breeders can sometimes mistake the sexes and need a couple of weeks before they are sure. For this reason, it is always wise for a person buying a pet, who has a distinct preference for a particular sex, to ask the opinion of an experienced person where this is possible.

SHOWS

Although the main UK show season does not start until the beginning of July and, in general for budgerigars, finishes at the beginning of December, shows of some kind are held for about nine months of the year. The smallest are table shows which are usually run by local societies for their members, at evening meetings. Sometimes these are restricted to beginner and novice sections only, or they may be run particularly for one variety. Frequently, judging competitions are run in conjunction with these shows. A well-known local judge is asked to place the exhibits in order and then the members are asked to judge the birds and the one whose result is nearest to that of the judge, is declared the winner.

The next grade of show is the *nest feather show* where breeders like to try out the show potential of the youngsters they have bred. Again, these are often run in conjunction with the clubs' meetings.

Young bird shows are usually the first of the clubs' major events. They are normally held before the open shows and concentrate on young birds which have to be rung with the current-year rings, but are no longer *barheads*. Some clubs treat the title literally and allow only current-year birds, while others include quite an extensive classification. Inexperienced fanciers often use these shows to seek advice on the quality of their stock and their youngsters.

Some societies organise *radius shows* which are a halfway stage between the young bird shows and the open shows. At these, exhibits are accepted from their own club members, wherever they live, and from the members of clubs within a given radius. This restricts the entry to a certain extent, giving more opportunity for local people to win the top honours.

Open shows are the next stage, and here they are open to all comers from any part of the country, which means that competition becomes keener. Some of the larger open shows become *championship shows* by virtue of the granting of *challenge certificate patronage* by the Budgerigar Society.

Above this level are the *area society shows* which have *challenge certificates*, both for any age and for breeders, and finally there is the *BS World Championship Show*, the Mecca of all dedicated breeders of budgerigars, whether as exhibitors or spectators.

SHOW CAGES

Show cages must comply with the specification of the ruling body in whatever country they are used. In Britain this is the Budgerigar Society. They should be painted a gloss black on the outside and with a semi-matt white paint inside. The wire front must be finished in white and should not show signs of chipped paintwork. The door to the standard water drinker must be fitted with an *ivorine label*. A list of licensed show-cage manufacturers is obtainable from the BS office, but many cage makers advertise in the fancy press, stating that they are licensed. Before buying cages, newcomers should ensure that they comply with the standard specifications, because if they do not, it is very likely that the exhibits will be disqualified by the judge.

For a show, the cage label showing the number of the class and the exhibit number should be positioned in the centre of the front rail. Any seed suitable for budgerigars can be used to cover the floor of the cage, but millet sprays may not be given until after judging has been completed. Clip-on drinkers are not permitted.

A beginner would be advised to buy some old show cages for use in the birdroom for training, working out pairings, moving birds from one place to another, and any job which requires a cage. New or reconditioned cages should be kept strictly for exhibiting.

To keep show cages used for exhibition purposes in tip-top condition and a credit to your birds, always wash and dry them when they

An important national show such as this one will attract thousands of entrants.

117

The spangle mutation

Two Capern's cards with grey and mauve budgerigars.

Spangle violet hen.

Spangle grey cock – notice the effect of this mutation on the spots, they can be tiny black centres on a mask coloured spot or mask coloured spots with a black outline.

Three show cages.

then be disturbed for the first ten days. After they have been given this period to settle down, they should each be given a few minutes in a show cage every day, just to ensure that they are familiar with the show cage and will be relaxed and unstressed when they come to be shown.

Three or four weeks before the show, the birds should be sprayed each day with tepid water. This should be done in the morning for preference, or at least at lunch time. Under no circumstances should they be left wet during the late evening, otherwise they could catch a chill or become vulnerable to a disease which their bodies could normally tolerate without harm. In really heavily polluted atmospheres it may be necessary to wash some of the birds, particularly those with light-coloured feathers (see *WASHING*). The first spray should be really heavy, to take off any dirt on the feathers. After that, a light spray will suffice and the birds will preen themselves, spreading oil from the preening gland over their feathers, making them shining and glossy. The spraying also tightens up any loose feathers and should be continued until about three days before the show.

At this time, the mask needs to be tidied. Any spots surplus to the statutory six should be removed with a pair of eyebrow tweezers. The bird should be held firmly in one hand and the feathers pulled out in the direction in which they are growing, one at a time. If the bird is particularly heavily spotted, it is best to remove the surplus spots in two sessions, returning the bird to the cage after the first batch has been taken out. Don't try to hurry this task, give yourself plenty of time and study the mask before taking out any feathers. It is very easy for a beginner to pull out the wrong feather by mistake and if one of the main spots is removed in error, it is going to be at least another three weeks before the bird will regrow the spot and be ready for showing. Practising this task on birds which you do not intend to show is a wise exercise, until the skill has been

are returned from a show. Avoid knocking them against each other, as the paintwork will chip. Store them out of sunlight, preferably covered up. Before they are taken to a show again, just give them a light polish on the outside.

For more than ten years, the general council of the Budgerigar Society has been considering the introduction of plastic show cages. These would have the advantage of being very easy to wash and keep clean, but it would mean every established competitor in the land would have to buy a complete set of new cages. As the established breeders are apt to take a team of 30 or more birds to a show, this would mean a very large item of expenditure. It would be a major decision to make the change to plastic cages, and thus it is still being considered.

SHOW PREPARATION

The decision as to which shows you will exhibit at needs to be taken at least six weeks before the first show. Potential show birds should be brought in and put into clean stock cages. Some breeders then pluck out any ragged or broken feathers, to give them time to regrow before the show date, but this procedure can, and does on occasion, result in the birds never growing that particular feather again. Other than to feed and water them, they should not mastered. Sometimes a beginner is so tense and fearful that his hands begin to sweat profusely and he spoils the feathering he has sprayed so assiduously during the previous weeks. At the first sign of this, he should stop trying to pluck the birds, return the bird he is holding to the stock cage, wash his hands and allow himself to calm down before continuing.

Once they have been plucked, the birds are ready for the show. The show cages should be given their final dust and polish and then filled with seed. It is wise to 'rough up' a small patch on the centre rail where the label will be placed, as this helps it to stick firmly. If this is not done, some cage labels can fall off the highly polished surface of the rail. The labels can be affixed before the birds are put into the cages, each bird being checked for its class before it is put into the cage or, alternatively, the birds can all be put in cages and then the labels attached to match up with the birds inside. Either way, great care should be taken that only current-year birds bred by the exhibitor are put into cages with labels for breeders classes, and that the labels are correct for colour and sex. A final check to see that the door is secured safely with the wire hook and that the desk catch is tight, and it's off to the show! If the show is due to last for two days, it is advisable to carry with you some millet sprays which can be soaked in water to be given to the birds after judging has been completed.

SHOW PROCEDURE FOR EXHIBITORS

When you have decided to enter a show, your first task should be to send for a schedule from the show secretary. Check the numbers of the classes you wish to enter, remembering that if you enter and show in a section above your own, you can then never return. If you are unsure or cannot understand the classification, ask for the advice of an experienced fancier. Fill in the form and send it, with any payment due, in plenty of time before the closing date for entries. When you receive your cage labels in return, check that they are correct. It is always possible for a busy show secretary to make an error under pressure.

The schedule will give the times between which your entries will be accepted and a final time after which entries will be refused. Make sure yours arrive well before that. Should you decide, for any reason, that you will not be taking your birds for exhibition, it is of great assistance to the show secretary if you notify him of the fact before the show.

When you arrive at the show hall, your birds will be taken to the booking-in point, the cage numbers will be checked and the birds taken away into the show hall. If you have decided not to show some of your exhibits, take the cage labels along to the show with you to show to the steward who will check in your birds. Unless you have arranged to help at the show, you will not see them again until after the birds have been judged and the exhibition is opened to the public.

When visiting the show, it is necessary, for your full enjoyment, to buy a catalogue to tell you the names of the owners of the birds, who is showing which variety, and their level of success. The catalogue and award sheet can give you a great deal of information even after the show is over, particularly if you make notes in the catalogue of your impressions of the different birds which have won. When you reach your own birds and perhaps find that they have won a prize, enjoy your success, but remember that the results at one show are often different from the results you would achieve at another. This is the time to use your catalogue to discover which exhibitors were showing that day and whether you have beaten any of the usually successful breeders, or whether they were all away at another show that particular week, allowing you the field to yourself. Sometimes it is impossible to have the award sheet ready for the exhibitors at the commencement of the show. Long-serving fanciers have usually had some experience of the amount of work involved in

Despite the smaller spots, this opaline cinnamon grey green cock has won many best of show awards.

Rare varieties

Normal grey green cock in peak show condition.

this methodical and arduous task and are tolerant of a little delay. Beginners would not make themselves popular by voluble impatience.

When the close of the show is announced, try not to rush, but take time to observe and learn the procedure for booking out. At most shows you are told to collect your entry forms and proceed to a certain exit, according to status or initials. You collect your cages and the cages are checked against your entry form by a steward before you are allowed to take them out of the hall.

When you arrive back in your birdroom with the birds, they should be run into a clean stock cage with which you have supplied seed and water and some millet sprays. If the birds have not eaten at the show – some of them become so excited that they forget to eat – they will soon start picking at the millet sprays. As you transfer the birds from show cage to stock cage, you may wish to take the ring numbers to record their successes or failures, but it is more important to observe whether they have lost body weight while they have been at the show, particularly if it was a two-day event. If this is apparent with any of the birds, then they need a minimum of two to three weeks of peaceful feeding until they are shown again.

The best part of show procedure for the keen fancier is that never seen by the public: the setting up of the show; preparing the staging and taking it down again after the public has left; rushing around with rosettes so that the hall will be colourful and ready before the public is allowed in; being part of the team at a successful show.

All beginners should offer to help at their local shows. Experience counts for less than the desire to learn and the willingness to work under the supervision of the more experienced. Once a newcomer has proved his desire to become part of the team, he is usually asked to steward at a show. This can be one of the most exciting moments for a beginner, as he sees a class of birds containing some of his own exhibits put before the judge. The

excitement can be overwhelming if he sees his birds put toward the premier position, but he has been told that he must never mention that he is showing in the class. If he is lucky and gains the first position, his bird will be judged against the winners in all the higher sections, for best of colour. This is where learning begins as a rule, as he sees the difference between beginner birds and those of the established champions. Sometimes, however, it must be admitted although very seldom, a beginner benches a bird which beats all the rest, and it is that hope which gives the great excitement to the mundane tasks of stewarding and staging dismantling for the new fancier.

SHOW PROCEDURE FOR JUDGES

Most shows in the UK are judged to the *certificate pattern*. This means that the judges will adjudicate first the juvenile section, choosing the best junior budgerigar which will take its place in the final line-up for its colour, then all the classes for birds of one colour or variety. If the colour being judged was light green, then all classes for light greens being exhibited by beginners, novices, intermediate, champions and the juvenile winner if it was light green are judged, and the first of each class retained. This is continued through all the colours and varieties. From each set of colour winners is chosen the best of its colour, the best breeder, the best opposite sex and the best opposite sex breeder. These results are recorded on the relevant cages and paperwork.

Now all the birds which have been awarded the title of best of colour any age are brought up before the judge, plus those chosen as best opposite sex of their colour, the best breeders and the opposite sex breeders. From these are chosen the best of each series for the titles of *best in show*, *best any age in show*, *best breeder in show* and their opposite sexes. Usually all activity ceases for a short time to enable all the stewards and helpers to watch these top places being judged.

As soon as the best bird has been

determined, there is a flurry of activity as all the winners are returned to their sections, so that the *best champion any age and breeder* and so on, throughout the five sections, can be chosen. Because the show may have accepted a number of patronages, it is necessary to find the highest-placed bird whose owner belongs to the various clubs which have given their patronage, therefore the overall position of the first prize winners from first to last throughout all the sections needs to be recorded by the judge. Judges can add to the exhibitors' enjoyment of the show if they remain after the opening of the show to the public so that exhibitors can ask for explanations as to why a particular bird did badly in its class or why another won top honours.

The judge finally reports to the show secretary or treasurer who pays his fee – at present the recommended UK amount is £7.50 – and any expenses for travelling or accommodation which he may have incurred.

SHOW REGISTER

Many long-standing champions can trace back their show registers for as many as 30 years or more. What details were kept differs with each individual. As an example, one from 1959 shows the name and date of the show, the cost of entry fees, cost of travel, description of each bird entered, together with its ring number and any awards it won. The number of birds in each class is entered and the name of the judge or judges. A typical entry gives some indication of the difference in costs today.

SHOW RULES

Most shows in the UK have an item printed in their schedules to say that they are run under the show rules of the Budgerigar Society and these rules can be found in the handbook. These have been only slightly modified over a period of almost 65 years. They are well known and accepted by all the major shows and exhibitors.

In addition, most schedules contain a list of rules for that particular show – usually the last time by which exhibits can be accepted and any other stipulation which the officials believe will ensure the smooth running of the show. Occasionally a problem can occur with smaller clubs or cage bird societies where that society has show rules which differ from those of the BS. If a problem or grievance occurs, the show officials will always try to resolve it. Most of the issues are caused by misunderstanding, as opposed to fanciers deliberately breaking show rules, and a quiet word with an official of the show will usually result in the matter being put right.

---

30 July, DERBY B&FBS

4 birds entered

1 L/G cock 9/58	AA 4th	11 entries
2 L/G hen 14/58	AA 1st	7 entries 2nd best beginner AA
3 Op Cinn G.G. hen 17/58	AA 1st	13 entries
4 Op L.Green cock 16/59	Breeder 1st	17 entries * best begin breeder

Entry fee	8/-
Train fare	16/-
Expenditure	£1/4/0
Prize money	£1/10/0
BS Prize money	15/0
Wooden Fruit Bowl	

Judge: W. Addey

A show register can be, as was this one, a plain note book, or they can be purchased with headings to allow for all the necessary information to be entered. They can be helpful to the newcomer as he learns more about the show potential of individual birds and they provide a fascinating history of trial, tribulations and successes for the fancier in future years.

Right: lacewing
cock showing
strong wing
pigment.

Budgerigars of quality

Head of an outstanding lacewing hen.

A selection of badges, spoons and other memorabilia issued over the years by the Budgerigar Society.

SHOW TRAINING

A budgerigar must be quite fearless and utterly at ease at a show for it to show itself to its best advantage. To achieve this, the first necessity is for the young birds to become familiar with the show cage. One way of achieving this is to attach an old show cage to the side of the stock cage in which the youngsters are kept when they leave their parents. Access can be through a hole the size of the show cage door, which has been removed, or round holes similar but larger than those they have been used to in the nest box. Seed, millet spray, seeding grasses and any other titbits they have learned to enjoy should be put into the show cage to entice the youngsters to enter. Soon they will go in and out of the show cages and sit on their perches without fear.

Another method is to have a number of show cages around the birdroom when cleaning it or carrying out other chores. The young birds are placed, individually, in the show cage for just a short period at a time. Once again, they can be given a millet spray to keep them occupied. It helps if the fancier talks to them and moves in front of the cage, just as will happen at a show. They will soon learn that there is nothing to fear in a show cage and that it is a temporary home from which they will be released back into the stock cage or flight with all their other companions.

Another thing they must learn, so that there will be no fear at the show, is to have their cages moved around from place to place. This can be done quite naturally, as the breeder judges his own birds to choose his team, if he continually moves one to the top of the line and another to the bottom, etc. This will simulate the behaviour of stewards as they move birds up and down the line for the judge at a show.

A judging stick might cause fear to a youngster when it is used for the first time, so it is sensible to use one for moving the bird from perch to perch. Alternating between wooden, plastic and metal sticks will ensure that there is no surprise whatever is used by the judge.

SOAKED SEED

Most seeds which have been soaked and are starting to sprout are welcomed by the birds, but they must be given in moderation. Soaking oats has been dealt with under *OATS*, but *canary seed* or *mixed millet seed* can also be used to advantage. These are soaked for two or three days, then drained and allowed to sprout. A small dish of these, given each day to the growing birds in the nursery flights, is both greatly appreciated and highly beneficial. If there is any sign of a stale, sour smell developing either during or after soaking, the seeds should be thrown away.

SOFTFOODS

When there are nestlings to be fed, softfood of some sort should be provided to the breeding pairs. A very nutritious form of softfood, which is highly recommended, is given under *FEEDING*, but several types of softfood are in current use by breeders. Wholemeal bread, soaked in milk and squeezed out, then sprinkled with a product containing wheatgerm or glucose, or even a little of each, is popular. Crumbled brown bread mixed with grated carrot and a type of dried yeast sold for budgerigars is another mixture often given, but this is lacking in animal protein. Wholemeal bread is the basis for most of the softfood offered, but, as with any additive to the basic diet, it should be given in small quantities because it contains salt, which, while a vital part of the diet, is not good in excess.

SOFT MOULT

This subject is dealt with fully under *MOULT*.

SPANGLES

The spangle mutation is the latest to be bred in Britain in any numbers. It first appeared in Victoria, Australia, in 1972 and was exported to Switzerland by a breeder who went to live there in the very early 1980s. When the breeder decided to return to Australia, he sold all his spangles to a German fancier. One of the leading British breeders saw this new variety and brought some back to Britain where they have proliferated and are now fairly popular. Not sufficient is known about the breeding pattern of spangles to state with any authority what the expectations can be. It is not sex-linked and appears to be of the dominant variety. When a spangle potential is carried by a normal bird, the spangling is visible. It reverses the colour of the normal pigmentation. Throat spots on a normal will appear as a coloured centre with a black border, instead of the usual black centre on a coloured border. This is repeated on all the other feathers; the markings become the colour of the original variety, and vice versa. It has been observed that the spangle gene seems to deepen the original colour of the bird, the greens or blues becoming a very vivid shade. They seem to be very fertile, especially the hens, and normals bred from spangles and then bred to another normal seem to carry this fertility with them.

When two spangle genes are present, in other words a double factor spangle, there appears to be another different colour change. The wings are almost devoid of markings and the body colour is clear and unbroken. They are often mistaken, by the uninitiated, for very good coloured clearwings.

Much work remains to be done on the genetics of this new mutation and at the moment the Australian standard for this bird is being followed for this variety until more information becomes available in Great Britain. In America, the mutation is so new that it is classed with their rare varieties.

SPECIALIST SOCIETIES

Five specialist societies exist in Britain, catering for a specific variety of birds. They are the Clearwing Budgerigar Breeders' Association which, as its name implies, was formed to promote the clearwing variety; the Variegated Budgerigar Club looks after the breeders of the pied varieties; the Rare Variety and Colour Budgerigar Society caters for the interests of all who are interested in birds not so often seen on the show bench. The birds covered vary from time to time as a variety either falls out of favour or becomes more popular. A list of the varieties currently covered is given under *RARE VARIETIES*. The Lutino and Albino Breeders' Society and the Crested Budgerigar Club have titles which are self-explanatory.

SPOTS

On all budgerigars whose standard asks that they carry spots, there should be six spots, low down on the

The unusual spots of the spangle variety.

The multi-spots of a barhead budgerigar.

mask. They should be round and evenly spaced, that is, the space between each spot should be equal to the size of the spot. The two outside spots are usually a little smaller than the four main ones and are partially covered by the cheek patches.

To improve the appearance of the bird for exhibition, it is permissible to remove any spots surplus to these six main spots – some birds can be so heavily spotted that they are carrying several dozen additional small spots or feathers which have part of a spot attached. There are two methods of removing these superfluous spots: they can be plucked out with an eyebrow tweezer, this method has been described under *SHOW PREPARATION*, or they can be cut off with sharp scissors. The surplus spots are lifted one at a time and the area of the feather showing any dark pigment is snipped off. This method has the advantage that these spots will not reappear until the bird moults out the feather that has been cut and regrows a new feather with a spot or part spot. Using the tweezer method, the feathers regrow in two to three weeks and will need trimming again.

SPRAYING

As well as removing any dust and grime, spraying improves the condition of the feathers by encouraging the bird to preen the feathers, coating each one with a minute quantity of natural oil. Spraying with tepid water is carried out for about three weeks before each show and always done early in the day to ensure that the birds never settle to roost while they are damp.

STANDARD OF EXCELLENCE

Each country has its standard of excellence for the budgerigar. Most of them are based on the British standard, but they differ slightly from country to country according to the way in which the budgerigar has developed in that land. The British standard, set by the Budgerigar Society is given under *IDEAL BUDGERIGAR*.

STARTING IN BUDGERIGARS

Many people see a show, read a book, or hear about the budgerigar fancy from a friend, and decide they would like to adopt this hobby which is, apparently, so very friendly and enjoyable. They go along to a show, talk to the exhibitors and, turning garage, spare bedroom or shed into their first birdhouse, they plunge in. With no knowledge, they listen to conflicting advice from all and sundry, spend a great deal of money on equipment and stock, change methods at the whim of every new contact and, after a couple of expensive years in which they have made little progress, they become discouraged and leave the hobby.

The newcomer needs guidance in

A spray with a fine nozzle, which produces a fine mist, is used for budgerigars.

his early years and the ideal situation would be to foster a relationship with an established fancier who is enjoying success on the show bench with his own-bred birds. This is not always possible, and very often the tiro will have to be prepared to help with the more menial tasks, but if such a friendship can be formed, the apprenticeship can be of value for the rest of the life of the newcomer. The would-be fancier who has just read a book, is hardly likely to know of a successful breeder and so should make his first step joining the local budgerigar or cage bird society. The address can often be obtained from a local library, or from the Budgerigar Society, or from any of the area societies listed under *USEFUL ADDRESSES*.

At the meetings of the club, as with any other hobby, there will be a diverse membership of those who will boast about their successes, even when they are but few, as well as many successful exhibitors who seldom mention their wins. The wise beginner will wait for a while before buying his stock or building, or converting a building to form his first birdroom. A lot can be learned just by listening to the speakers and members. Breeding exhibition budgerigars with any degree of success is not a hobby which can be rushed. It needs patience and dedication, but the rewards in lasting friendships and an absorbing new lifestyle are something which most established fanciers consider well worth the effort. Once contact has been made with a fancier who is genuinely successful and who has offered his help and guidance, there are a few vital rules to be followed:

Always make arrangements before arriving at your new friend's aviary. People who are established in the hobby usually have many friends and callers. If you continually arrive unannounced, you will become upopular.

Always arrive on time. This applies to any aviary you would like to visit. Remember that the breeder probably works during the week, and has many chores to do at the weekend, as well as showing his birds to a number of other people who have also made appointments.

If you have made an appointment to visit an aviary, which for some reason you are unable to keep, always telephone as soon as possible to advise the fancier that you will not be coming.

Don't overstay your welcome. Most fanciers live for budgerigars. They will talk about them endlessly, will help and advise you on all aspects of the hobby, will recommend those who are best able to assist you with your birdroom, stock, or whatever your requirements may be, but they are usually busy people and will indicate when they can spend no more time with you on that occasion.

The budgerigar fraternity is a small world. Your reputation will spread quite quickly, first through the local community and then, as you travel further afield, among fanciers countrywide. Make certain that it is a reputation for courtesy and willingness to learn. It will not be many years before you could be an established fancier and then it will be your turn to give your time to help beginners find their place in a lifetime's hobby.

When you have decided what sort of birdroom you will need and what stock you will require, there are helpful hints under *BIRDROOMS* and *BUYING BUDGERIGARS*.

STATUS

Show status is the section in which a breeder is showing. If under sixteen years of age, and not living in the same house as a breeder showing in a higher section, he can show in the juvenile classes. His status is therefore *junior*. The first status for adults is *beginner*, followed by *novice*, *intermediate* and then *champion*. The rules for showing in these sections are given under their respective headings. In America and some other countries, there is no beginner class and a newcomer enters as a novice. The rules for moving from one section to another are also different. For example, in America, the novice cannot simply choose to show in a higher section, he must first achieve his requisite number of wins.

STUD REGISTRATION

For a small annual fee, a distinctive name for a stud can be registered with the Budgerigar Society office and this name cannot then be used by any other fancier or partnership. Names for studs are very often derived from the name of the house of the fancier, or the street in which he or she lives, for example 'The Castle Stud' for someone living in Castle Avenue.

SWEATING NEST BOXES

This term is a misnomer used to describe a nest box which becomes wet, with the sawdust becoming quite soggy. It is the hen which does the 'sweating'. Sometimes this is caused because she has a very high intake of water when breeding and this cannot, or certainly should not, be controlled in any way. Sometimes the wetness is caused, again by a high intake of water, when the hen's droppings become very wet. The material of the nest box has a significant influence on this condition. Softwood is the best material to use to minimise it. Ventilation of the nest box, by drilling holes near to the top, is another method of controlling excessive wetness. The sawdust, or other filling of the boxes of hens, which seems to produce this extra moisture, should be changed more frequently. When refilling with clean sawdust while small chicks are in the nest, it should be ensured that the new sawdust is not stored in a place where it will be icy cold and give a shock to the youngsters. If necessary, it should be put near a radiator to warm.

T

TALKING

'Will it talk?' This must be the question most frequently asked of the breeder or pet-shop owner when someone buys a budgerigar, and the answer should be 'That's up to you.'

The stories that there is such a thing as a 'talking strain' of budgies, or that cocks will talk and hens will not, are all fallacies. Budgerigars are natural mimics. If they are kept alone, without any of their own kind to 'speak' to, they will mimic other sounds they hear. An example of this was a budgerigar owned by a lady who was quite deaf. Because she could not hear, she made no attempt to teach her budgie to talk, but anyone who called to see her, especially anyone with any knowledge of budgies, was horrified to hear the little thing coughing so badly that it appeared to have the greatest difficulty in hanging on to the perch or drawing the next breath. One couple, budgie breeders themselves, were so upset at the plight of the bird that they persuaded a friend who was a vet to accompany them on a visit to see if he could give the bird any treatment to relieve the cough. The owner was most amused when they were able to convey to her their concern. She explained that she suffered very badly from asthma and the budgie would mimic not only her terrible coughing and wheezing, but also her attitude as she bent over, grasping the table for support – hence his habit of appearing to be hanging on to the perch.

If you are prepared to give your budgie the time it takes to teach a word, a sentence, and eventually whole verses or nursery rhymes, it will repay you by giving you hours and hours of amusement as you listen to its repertoire. One, a hen, used to sit on her owner's spectacles, gaze into her eyes and say, 'Oh, I do love you'. Despite constant repetition, this seldom failed to bring tears to the eyes of the dear old lady who owned the bird, although all that it was doing was repeating what it must have heard many, many times.

The first words are important. Once a budgerigar has begun to copy a word, it quickly adds to its repertoire, but it often takes quite a while before it masters its first couple of words. It is best to choose something quite simple to start, which is why 'pretty boy' is so popular. It is best if one person, preferably female, because the female voice is pitched higher than the male, takes on the task of teaching the first words, so that the bird is not confused. If time is of the essence, then a tape recorder can be used. If the teacher records, say, 'pretty boy', on a tape for as many times as the tape will allow, this can be played near the cage, even when no one is in the house. Once the bird has learned the first phrase, another can be added, but each phrase should always be learned thoroughly before another is added. Nursery rhymes are popular and, in general, consist of simple words, but a budgerigar in Wales is on record as being able to say 'Llanfairpwllgwyn-gyllgogerychwrndrobwllllantisilio gogogoch!'.

A very useful thing to teach a budgie is its name and address. More than one pet who has escaped has been returned to its owner after chirping its name and address to its amazed finder.

One word of warning. A budgie will not talk if it has other budgies to talk to. It must be kept as a single pet for it to learn to speak, and it will be very unlikely to talk if training is not started before it is about four months old. It has been known, but the likelihood is fairly remote.

As well as speech, budgies can be taught to whistle – a wolf whistle being a typical example. In this case, it is a man who is usually the better teacher. A tune should be chosen which has a simple opening phrase and this is repeated again and again until the bird can remember and reproduce it with ease. Once this has been achieved, a new section is added and both are always whistled together, until the bird has learned the two, then another and another until the whole tune is mastered. No musical box can give the same thrill as a budgie greeting you with a happy tune when you return to your home, and it will be a source of constant amusement to your callers.

TAMING

Confidence is the secret of taming a budgerigar. The finest form of training is done as soon as the baby leaves the nest box, and pet breeders can almost ensure being able to sell their youngsters if they, or one of their family, is prepared to spend the time and take the trouble to play with the baby budgerigars and hand feed them until they have no fear whatsoever of people and hands. Just as the chicks once scrambled back into the nest box, so they will scramble through a hole made with finger and thumb, and if they are used to sitting on a hand and eating seed or millet spray from it, they will have no fear when a hand is put into their new pet cage.

Because a pet cage is very different from the stock cage from which most budgies are taken, they should be left alone for a few hours to acclimatise themselves with their new surroundings. It is best not to have a swing in the cage for the first day or two, so that they can learn to fly confidently to a perch, knowing that they can land on it safely. The swing, if there is one, can be introduced once the bird feels quite safe in the cage. Open dishes on the bottom of the cage for seed, or even seed sprinkled over the bottom of the cage is advisable for the first two or three days, until the baby bird is used to eating out of the new seed containers. If the new owner has the patience to sit with his or her hand inside the cage, holding a millet spray, the bird, even if it has not been reared as a pet, will begin to eat the seeds from it after a while and the more this is done, the sooner the bird becomes used to, and eventually starts to sit on, the hand. A budgerigar cannot be said to be tame until it will hop onto the owner's hand with the same alacrity as it will hop onto a perch. Once it has lost its initial fear of a hand being put into its cage, it can be coaxed onto the hand by putting the finger just underneath its chest, in front of its legs and slowly pressing the finger backwards. As it must perch, and it can no longer hold on to the real perch, it automatically moves onto the finger, hardly realising that its perch has changed.

Be careful, when drinking hot liquids, not to let your inquisitive budgie burn its tongue – remember, it is not used to hot food or drink.

Some birds are far more nervous than others and will fly wildly if someone approaches their cage at the beginning. All movements should be slow and unhurried, and the owner should talk to the bird as he or she approaches the cage. A little patience at this stage will be well rewarded later on. Once the budgerigar is hand tame, and will hop onto a finger automatically when it is put inside the cage, the bird can be allowed out into the room – after any open or electric fire has been covered and the curtains have been closed to prevent it from flying into the unfamiliar glass pane. Slowly it can be taught to perch on a shoulder, by being transferred from finger to shoulder, or to another person's shoulder. Soon, it will accept a shoulder as another of its perches and it will fly from cage to shoulder as soon as it is allowed out. The tamer a budgie becomes, the more responsibility the owner has to ensure that he or she *never* leaves the house with the bird still on a shoulder, and *never* opens the cage before first checking that all doors and windows are closed. So

much heartbreak has been caused by a bird being taken outdoors, or getting out, and then being startled and flying off wildly. Once out into the outside world it is lost, frightened and often flies a long distance before alighting, by which time it is far away from home.

Unless a hawk or other hunting bird is in the vicinity, the ordinary garden birds do not attack the lone budgerigar, but it has no knowledge of cats and often falls victim to them, and in any case it has been used to eating only seed and there is very little seed in the wild except seeding grasses which are only available at certain times of the year and, unfortunately, have often been treated with sprays which could be lethal. The escaped bird is unlikely to survive for long.

TICKING
Ticking, frosting and flecking are all words used to describe excess *melanin* which causes marks on top of the head of budgerigars. It is a fault in show birds and is penalised by the judges. An illustration of this will be found under the heading *FLECKING*.

This fault is a problem because it is hereditary, and it is therefore wiser not to breed with birds which are flecked. Although by judicious breeding the fault can apparently be made to disappear, it can, and often is, carried by the offspring in a recessive and hidden form and will reappear in future generations. Unless the birds are of otherwise superb quality, it is better not to use flecked birds in the breeding team, and no one but the really experienced breeder should use them under any circumstances.

TOE NAILS
When in the nest box, the toes of baby budgerigars may become fouled by excreta and often, by the time the nest box is examined, this has become quite hard. It should not be picked off while hard, as it is very easy to pull off a toe nail. As well as causing the bird some pain and disfiguration, the bird will thus be spoiled for showing. The foot should be soaked in warm water for a few

seconds to soften the excreta which can then be removed with a soft cloth.

Like human nails, the bird's toe nails grow. Provided it has access to some sort of rough surface and has something other than round dowelling for perches, normal moving around will wear away the small amount of growth, but sometimes a hen, sitting for a long time in a nest box, will grow excessively long toe nails. These are a nuisance for the bird and can also accidentally pierce an egg, causing the chick inside to die before it is born. Pets are prone to overgrown toe nails, partly because they usually live to a ripe old age and partly because they lead a less active life than a bird in an aviary. One thing which will help to prevent this is a piece of old brick left in the corner of the cage. They use this as a form of grit and for entertainment in scraping it away to nothing, and as they hold it in one foot, or press a foot against it to be able to pull it apart more successfully, it keeps their nails trimmed.

If toe nails do become too long, they have to be cut. This causes no more pain to the budgie than it does to the human. The foot should be held up to the light where it will be seen that blood vessels grow part of the way down the toe and then there is a part which is purely nail and is devoid of any blood vessels. Cut a little at a time with sharp nail clippers, holding the toe up to the light each time to make sure you will not cut the living part. Continue with each of the toes in turn. Once cutting has been commenced, the nails will grow quicker than they did before, and so will need to be cut on a regular basis.

If, by some unfortunate chance, the nail is cut too deep and bleeding occurs, a little styptic pencil will often stop the bleeding. This should be followed by a drop of salt water to remove the silver nitrate from the pencil. The bird should then be kept quiet in its cage for a while to prevent the bleeding starting again or, if it has not been stopped, to give the blood time to clot and stop of its own accord.

TOYS

Budgies are naturally playful and, even in flights with many others, they love to swing on home-made swings (see *EQUIPMENT*). They also make their own playthings from feathers which have moulted, millet spray stalks and greenfood which has been eaten down to the stalks.

Pets have no other birds with which to play and appreciate toys with which to amuse themselves. Owners should check these toys just as carefully as they check those for children's use, because the clanger from a bell which is loose can be swallowed by the budgie just as easily as a child will swallow a loose bead, while a piece of wire sticking out can cause the same damage to either. Mirrors are almost a necessity for a happy budgie and a particular favourite is a mirror at the bottom of a shallow dish filled with water. The budgie will splash around

A rotating swing is a favourite of budgerigars. This example is sold commercially, but they are also easy to make for oneself.

135

Budgerigars like to climb ladders but make certain that the bird cannot become stuck between the rungs.

happily in this – but splash is the operative word! The dish should be placed on newspaper or an old cloth, otherwise most of the water will land on the carpet.

Kelly dolls are another favourite and provided the owner has the patience to pick them up from the floor a hundred times a day, the budgie will cheerfully continue to throw them over. Care must be taken that the rungs of ladders are not so far apart that the budgie can get stuck between them.

If shop-bought toys are not available, several cotton reels strung tightly on a string are well received, although it is often necessary to renew the string which will be chewed through. Another item enjoyed by most budgies is a shallow tray on which have been placed a few glass marbles. The bird will spend hours on end throwing these out onto the floor.

TRACE MINERALS

In addition to the proteins, carbohydrates and fats which the birds obtain from seed and the various additives which are given to them, they also require a small quantity of certain trace minerals for their health and well being. Most of these are contained in canary and

millet seed, but there is often insufficient calcium and iodine in the normal diet.

Iodine can be given in the form of iodine nibblets, but because of the budgerigar's habit of tearing at any object which is friable, a great deal of these are wasted. Pet stores stock a harder, larger block containing iodine which, although marketed for pigeons, is ideal for budgerigar breeding cages or flights, though rather too large for the pet cage. Iodine can also be given in the water, but in quite minute quantities, or a few drops of a well-known iodine-based disinfectant can be added to the water. Alternatively, millet sprays can be soaked in a weak solution of iodine-treated water before being fed to the birds.

Oystershell and limestone grit are the most readily available forms of calcium, but Vitamin D is also necessary for the absorption of calcium by the body. Vitamin D is manufactured by the body when it is exposed to sunlight, but as few breeding cages obtain any direct sunlight, it is vital, particularly at the time when calcium is needed by the hen for making eggshell, and by the chicks to make strong bones, to give extra Vitamin D. This is available in cod liver oil which can be mixed with the seed given.

TREES

A tree-planted aviary is not suitable for budgerigars, or to be more accurate, budgerigars are not suitable for a tree-planted aviary. Their habit of tearing to shreds anything which can be torn is hardly conducive to the survival of trees and plants. However, they love to have branches of trees to play in and with and to eat the leaves, bark and, if soft enough, the wood itself. Most of the British trees are suitable, but yew, laburnum and other poisonous species must be avoided at all costs. The favourites are the fruit trees, unless one is lucky enough to be able to grow a eucalyptus tree. In Australia, where the eucalyptus trees grow wild, budgies descend upon them like locusts, eating leaves, bark and wood and often nesting in the trunks of dead trees.

The few fanciers who have succeeded in growing eucalyptus in the UK find the birds attack any newly picked branches with great enthusiasm.

TYPE

Type embodies the whole image of the bird. It depicts the image of a guardsman on parade, embracing every aspect. The bird should be standing on the perch with a backline of 30 degrees from the vertical, the head must be held in a bold, confident manner, extending the apparent length of the bird. The wings must be held tightly to the body with the tips of the wings just cushioning the tail. If the bird has a very slight, very gentle dip in the back line, it does seem to give it a more desirable stance and to make it look more alert, but, when viewed from either side, the line must be clean and sweeping from head to tail with the maximum width around the breast and shoulder area. Even if the bird has long feathering, it should be tight and in place. Coarse-feathered birds are often criticised for lack of type because the feathers, being long, tend to be loose.

Balance is an integral part of type. Everything must be in proportion. The body must be in proportion to the head, the mask in proportion to the head, the spots in proportion to the mask and the beak in proportion to the face. A budgerigar with a small body and big head can look like a hanging parrot; with a big body and small head, it resembles a pigeon slumped across the perch. A really well-balanced budgerigar is a thing of beauty – it is a bird with type!

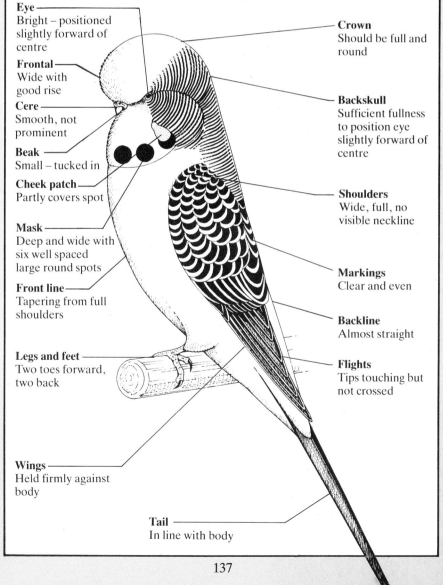

Eye
Bright – positioned slightly forward of centre

Frontal
Wide with good rise

Cere
Smooth, not prominent

Beak
Small – tucked in

Cheek patch
Partly covers spot

Mask
Deep and wide with six well spaced large round spots

Front line
Tapering from full shoulders

Legs and feet
Two toes forward, two back

Wings
Held firmly against body

Crown
Should be full and round

Backskull
Sufficient fullness to position eye slightly forward of centre

Shoulders
Wide, full, no visible neckline

Markings
Clear and even

Backline
Almost straight

Flights
Tips touching but not crossed

Tail
In line with body

137

U

UNDERSHOT BEAK

This is a deformity of the beak caused by food being caught under the upper hook of the mandible of chicks in the nest box. As this hardens, the lower mandible is unable to fit underneath. Unless the top beak is cleaned regularly, the soft food sets like concrete and eventually the lower mandible passes over instead of under the top

A case of an undershot beak.

hook. Not only does this disfigure the bird, but it also causes difficulty in cracking seed. To assist the bird in eating properly, the lower mandible needs to be trimmed. This is best carried out with strong, sharp nail clippers and care must be taken not to cut into the blood supply. If the bird is held up to the light, the end of the blood vessel region can be seen quite clearly and any cutting must not go into or beyond this area. It is best to take off the excess a little at a time, checking regularly to ensure that the bloodline has not been reached. Beginners are recommended to ask the help of an experienced fancier the first time this operation is necessary, as it is easier to learn by watching it being done.

USEFUL ADDRESSES

The newcomer to budgerigars is often at a loss where to look for help, where to find the address of his local club, or of other fanciers in his area. The Budgerigar Society, or area societies in Britain, and the ruling bodies in other countries can supply these details. The addresses of these bodies are given below:

AMERICA – The American Budgerigar Society, Secretary, Mrs Natalie Pittman, 1704 Kangaroo, Kileen, Texas 76543, USA, or Chairman, Ms Ermafern Collins, 304 Kellogg, Dallas Centre, Idaho 50063, USA.

AUSTRALIA – Budgerigar Society of South Australia. Mr R. Deslandes, No 7 West Street, Ascot Park, South Australia, 5043.

BELGIUM – Ornitho Club Seraing, 2 Rue des Steches, 4230 Horion Hosemont, Belgium.

EIRE – Eire Budgerigar Society, Hon. Sec. Mr H. Harrison, Rocky Valley Lodge, Kilmacanugue, Co Wicklow, Eire.

FRANCE – Club Nationale Des Oiseaux Exotiques. Mr J. Barre, Lot No. 17, Champ de Rochefort, 16400 Puymoyen, France.

GERMANY – Austauschzentrale der Vogel-liebhaber und -züchter Deutschlands E.V., General Sekretar: G. Wittenbrock, 286 Osterholz-Scharmbeck, vor Der Elm 1, Munchen 246 74 807, Germany.

Redaktion D.S.V. Nachrichten, Schildsheider Str., 4006 Erkrath 2, Germany.

JAPAN – The Japan International Budgerigar Association, Secretary Mr M. Takezawa, 16-24-2 Chome, Nozato, Nishiyodogawa, Osaka 555, Japan.

The Japan Budgerigar Club, Mr H. Nakayama, 3-6 Nishiyama 1 Chome, Kashlwa Si, Chiba Ken, 277 Japan.

NEW ZEALAND – The Budgerigar Society of New Zealand, Secretary: Mrs C. R. Carlyon, P.O. Box 54-077, Plimmerton, Wellington, New Zealand.

SWEDEN – The Swedish Budgerigar Society, Secretary Mr U. Thorn, Bjornidegrand 11, S 162 46 Vallingby, Sweden.

UK – The Budgerigar Society, 49/53 Hazelwood Road, Northampton NN1 1LG.

Clearwing Budgerigar Breeders' Association, c/o M. Freemantle, 15 Northcourt Avenue, Reading.

Crested Budgerigar Club, c/o Mr and Mrs Risebrow, 59 Glencoe Rd, Ipswich, Suffolk.

Lancashire, Cheshire and North Wales Budgerigar Society, c/o R. James, 14 Hadfield Close, Widnes, Cheshire.

Lincolnshire and East Anglia Budgerigar and Foreign Bird Society, c/o Mrs S. Freshney, Flat 4, Lagoon Way, Lilliput, Nr Poole, Dorset.

London and Southern Counties Budgerigar Society, c/o S. Stephenson, 2, Shalmsford Street, Chartham, Canterbury, Kent.

Lutino and Albino Breeders' Society, c/o J. Bancroft, 14 Whitehouse Drive, Long Stratton, Norfolk.

Midland Budgerigar Association, c/o Mrs O. Jordan, 53 Worcester Lane, Four Oaks, Sutton Coldfield, West Midlands.

Northern Budgerigar Society, c/o V. Scott, 27 Park Road South, Chester-le-Street, Durham.

Rare Variety and Colour Budgerigar Society, c/o C. Putt, 124 Stonewell Crescent, Whitestone, Nuneaton, Warwicks.

Scottish Budgerigar Society, c/o A. R. Cameron, 98 Auchenlodment Road, Elderslie, Renfrewshire.

South Midlands Budgerigar and Foreign Bird Society, c/o Mrs L. Stephens, 20 Reynards Road, Old Welwyn, Herts.

Variegated Budgerigar Club, c/o Mr & Mrs J. Suddell, 'Southdene' 218 Noak Hill Road, Billericay, Essex.

Welsh Budgerigar Society, c/o J. V. Blackey, 84 Cherry Grove, Derwen Fawr, Swansea.

Western Counties Budgerigar and Foreign Bird Society, c/o Mr & Mrs A. Winter, 3 Glanfield Terrace, Limmington, Yeovil, Somerset.

Yorkshire Budgerigar Society, c/o E. Geary, 24 Pheasant Bank, Rossington, Doncaster.

V

VARIEGATED
This term is used to describe the irregular patches of colour on the body and wings and the lack of colour in the flight feathers of the pied variety of budgerigars.

VARIETIES
There are now a large variety of budgerigars obtainable. The *normal* varieties include light, dark and olive green, grey green, light, dark and olive yellow, grey yellow, yellow suffused, skyblue, cobalt, mauve, violet, grey, and white suffused. The same list of colours is available in the *opaline*, *cinnamon* and the *opaline cinnamon* varieties. The next series are the *greywings* which come in all the basic colours followed by *opaline greywings*. In the *clearwing* variety there are yellow-wing light, dark and olive greens, yellow-wing grey greens, white-wing skyblues, whitewing cobalts, whitewing mauves, whitewing violets and whitewing greys. The whole series of colours is repeated in the *fallow* variety, the *dominant* and *recessive pieds*, the *clearflights, crests* and the new *spangles*. In addition to these there are *albinos, lutinos, lacewings yellows* and *whites* and *dark-eyed yellows and whites*. There are well over 100 different varieties from which to choose, whereas at the beginning of the century, the choice was light green or yellow.

VENTILATION
Adequate ventilation is an absolute essential in the birdroom for the well being of your stock, while draughts must be avoided at all costs. The recommended form of ventilation is a series of mouse-proof air vents fitted into the walls low down, preferably beneath the bottom layer of breeding cages, combined with louvres or an extractor fan fitted as high in the birdroom as possible. Whichever is used must be fitted with a birdproof screen across the

opening just in case any of the birds escape from the cages into the main room. This ensures a constant flow of fresh air which also helps to carry out some of the dust.

VERMIN

The urine and droppings of rats and mice are poisonous to the birds. If vermin are present in an aviary, seed, sawdust, shavings, cuttlefish, anything with which the birds will come in contact, can be fouled by their urine without the breeder being able to see any trace. If any of these items are fed to the budgerigars, or used anywhere where the birds can chew or nibble at them, the results could be disastrous. Prevention, in this case, is far better than cure. When the birdhouse is being built, every precaution should be taken to make the building mouse-proof (if it is mouse-proof it will certainly be rat-proof). Small-mesh wire should be fitted over every means of entrance. Seed should never be left around in half-opened sacks, but stored in plastic dust bins or similar containers. No foodstuff should be stored in dark, fairly inaccessible cupboards at floor level, but kept on shelves, in sight. Feeding trays are best mounted on plastic or smooth-sided material so that mice cannot crawl up. Seed should never be purchased from a shop where open sacks are left around, it is far better to buy a complete sack and store it until it is needed. If, despite every precaution, traces of vermin are found in the birdroom, they must be eradicated as quickly as possible. There are a number of patent traps for this purpose, which are safe for birds, advertised in the fancy press. Poison bait is *not* a good idea.

VITAMINS

Budgerigars need vitamins, as do any other form of living creatures, but they need them in minute quantities. Unfortunately some breeders, in their desire to ensure that their birds have every additive which can be given, overdose their birds with vitamins, sometimes with unhappy results. An excess of Vitamin A has been blamed for some forms of *'going light'*. Vitamin D, in excess, can cause enlarged joints and constipation, among other things. If the diet consists of good wholesome seed, which has been treated with cod liver oil emulsion during the moult and breeding season, an adequate supply of greenfood and mixed grits, which contain oystershell and limestone, this should take care of the birds' vitamin requirements. Where greenfood is not available, or not supplied for some reason, a few drops of Abidec or a similar multivitamin product can be added to the water, but this should be added at only about five drops to 0.5 litre (1 pt).

Budgerigars obtain Vitamin B12 by eating their own dried droppings, but after any illness which has caused diarrhoea, these are not available, nor is Vitamin B12 present in the droppings if antibiotics have been administered for a period. This shortage can be made up by adding something like Cytacon to the water at the rate of one teaspoonful per 0.5 litre (1 pt). The other vitamin lacking in most natural foods is Vitamin E, which is very beneficial during the breeding season. A small quantity of bee pollen added to the softfood fills this need.

W

WASHING

In country areas, or places where the air is clean and clear, there is seldom any need to wash budgerigars for showing, but in cities or highly polluted atmospheres, spraying is not really sufficient to clean the feathers and the birds, particularly the lighter varieties, such as lutinos, albinos, clearwings and lacewings, do need to be washed. This should always be carried out in the morning, to allow the birds all day to dry naturally. Most breeders choose a weekend for this rather lengthy task. The birds are washed about a month before the show and then put into clean stock cages to dry. As they are then kept indoors in the stock cages, light spraying will keep their feathers in a clean condition, ready for the show.

To wash a bird, or birds, three bowls are required. The first contains warm water and baby shampoo, the second plain warm water, and the third warm water with the addition of a few drops of plume conditioner (this is optional). The bird is held so that its eyes are protected and the washing carried out with an old soft shaving brush, always brushing in the direction in which the feathers grow. Should there be any staining around the beak, or dried blood spots on top of the head, an old soft toothbrush can be used to remove them. Once the head and body have been washed, each wing should be spread out gently and washed on both sides. The bird is then dipped into the second bowl. The water must not be allowed to come over the head, but only very gently dripped over the head and beak areas. Finally, the bird is dipped into the third basin of water in the same way. Excess water can be blotted off with an old towel before the bird is released into the clean stock cage.

WATER

Although budgies do not drink a great deal, a supply of *fresh* water must always be available. With an automatic system, it is assured that the water is just as fresh as the water drunk by humans, because it comes straight from the tap. If this is not available, then the water should be changed every day. In cages, the most convenient form of water container is the fountain drinker which consists of a clear plastic tube with an open end. When filled, a cap with a drinking spout is fitted and the fountain turned upside down. The force of gravity fills the drinking spout, allowing the birds to drink at will. Care must be taken not to fit

The correct way to hold a budgerigar when bathing it.

A hen budgerigar with a very young chick. It will be fully weaned at about the age of six weeks.

the cap with the cut out piece meeting the cut out on the tube, otherwise the water would run out immediately it was fitted to the cage, leaving the bird with only the few drops remaining in the spout. If the spout becomes contaminated with droppings or seeds, the water very quickly becomes foul and should be changed immediately.

For flights or garden aviaries, open dishes are the usual vessels used. The water should be no more than 4 cm (1½ in) deep because the birds use the water dishes as baths and if one became too wet and unable to fly it could get into difficulties, or even drown. Birds will bathe in any temperature; it is a form of recreation for them and appears to do them no harm, even in mid-winter, in fact, it tends to tone up the feathers.

Thought must be given to the position of water dishes. They should not be placed under perches where they could become fouled by droppings, or where husks from the seed are likely to fly into them. Ideally, they should be placed on a pedestal, higher than the food dishes, in a shaded area which will minimise evaporation from the sun and reduce the growth of algae. Glazed dishes are recommended because they are easy to keep clean. In a garden aviary, they can even be washed and replenished using the garden hose.

WEANING

Baby budgerigars are usually self-supporting at the age of six weeks and can then be taken away from their parents. If possible, it is as well to take them away in batches, rather than singly. When half a dozen or more youngsters from different families are ready to be separated from their parents and put in a stock cage together, the more forward babies teach the others how to crack seed with ease. Some breeders like to put an old and reliable cock into the cage with the youngsters as a venerable teacher, but this can have its difficulties if the cock begins to attack one or more of the youngsters. Generally, the chicks manage quite well on their own.

During the first few weeks of their independent life, the babies should be given the same additives that they have been used to in the breeding cage. Soaked oats, soaked mung beans and softfood are always welcomed, as are millet sprays. Chickweed is greeted with delight if it is available, and another very good source of vitamins is spinach.

If, within 24 hours, it is observed that a baby is not feeding and the crop feels empty, it can be put back with its parents or with foster parents, but a close watch must be kept on it for a couple of hours to make certain that the parents do not reject and attack it. If this happens and the parents will not feed it, and the baby is unable to feed itself, the breeder will have to try hand feeding (see *HAND FEEDING*). Fortunately, at this stage of development, hand feeding is seldom necessary for more than a day or two and is well worth a try if it saves the youngster. A bird this old can take food from a spoon quite easily and does not need a brooder. In a show cage with seed on the floor, it will soon learn to crack its own food, especially if another, more forward baby is kept in the same cage.

WINGS
The wings of a show budgerigar should be 9.5 cm (3¾ in) long. They should be carried just above the cushion of the tail and should not be crossed. Wings which cross over each other is one of the commonest faults and one for the beginner to avoid when buying his first stock because it is a fault which is difficult to eradicate. Another fault, which makes the bird look most unattractive, is a habit of dropping the wings, or sometimes just one wing, down at the side of the body, looking as if the bird is too tired to hold them up.

Wings, carried correctly, should be neatly folded and look as if they are part of the body.

WRONG CLASS
Nothing is more frustrating for the newcomer to budgerigar shows than to arrive to find his cages marked W/C, or wrong class. When placing the birds, the judge also watches to see that each bird corresponds with the description of the class and if it does not, marks the cage label W/C and the bird is disqualified. It is very easy for a beginner, with a few blue birds, to see classes on the schedule for 'skyblue, cobalt or mauve'. As he has skyblues and cobalts with yellow faces, he enters them in the blue class. What he has failed to do is to read the rest of the classification which tells him that there is a separate class for yellowface blues and when he arrives at the show he finds his birds disqualified. Another mistake often made is to enter a number of birds, some adult and others bred in the current year, and then stick the cage labels for green breeders onto the green any-age birds, and so on. Again, they would be marked W/C. Beginners need to learn what the more experienced have learned, often the hard way, that the classifications on a schedule must be read very, very carefully and the cage labels checked before they are taken to a show to make certain that the right birds are in the right cages.

It is very easy for a beginner to mistake an opaline for a normal, not to notice the cinnamon markings, to mistake a grey green for an olive green, and so on, particularly if the cages are being filled in a fairly dark birdroom. Check and check again is the rule to be followed here. If the new exhibitor is unsure, even after checking, that he has labelled all the birds correctly, the steward or secretary checking in the birds at the show will help him or arrange for someone experienced to do so. However, if help is necessary, the exhibitor should be certain to arrive early, because, in the last minute rush before judging, the officials will have no time to spare.

X Y Z

X CHROMOSOME

X is the sex chromosome. The cock carries two and the hen one. Several of the varieties of budgerigars are *sex-linked*, which means that their potential can only be carried on the X chromosome. This gives the effect that if a hen is carrying that potential, she displays it visually. If, for example, she is carrying a potential for the lutino variety on her single X chromosome, she will be a lutino. If she is not, she cannot carry the lutino potential in hidden or split form because it cannot be on her other chromosome which is a Y chromosome. As the cock carries two X chromosomes, he can be split for lutino or whichever sex-linked variety he is carrying.

YELLOWFACE

The yellowface variety of budgerigars is unusual in several respects. There are two different types, called *mutant I* and *mutant II*. The mutant I birds are those on which the BS colour standard is based. They are blue birds with yellow faces and masks, and the yellow cuts off immediately beneath the mask. In the mutant II variety, the yellow runs right through the body, changing the blue to turquoise. There is a school of thought which states that these birds are not blue birds at all, but green birds in which the yellow-producing pigment has been partially suppressed. Their mode of inheritance is also unusual, because if two single factor yellowface blues are mated together, they can produce perfectly ordinary looking whitefaced blues, but 50 per cent of these will, theoretically, be double factor yellowface blues and when mated to an ordinary whiteface blue, will produce all yellowface young. This can be absolutely amazing to a breeder who has no knowledge of the parentage of his stock of blues.

YELLOWS

Yellows, being the recessive form of green, come in the same range of colours: light, dark, olive and grey yellow. In addition there is a *suffused variety* which also comes in light, dark and olive shades. These birds are suffused with a very dilute shade of the colour being masked. Another variety of yellow is the dark-eyed clear yellow which is pure yellow throughout, including clear yellow wings. At a quick glance, the bird could be taken for a pale-coloured lutino until the dark eyes are observed.

ZYGOTES

A zygote is the first cell of a chick, which contains the necessary double set of chromosomes.

144